50 MEDIEVAL FINDS FROM THE PORTABLE ANTIQUITIES SCHEME

Michael J. Lewis

First published 2018

Amberley Publishing
The Hill, Stroud
Gloucestershire, GL5 4EP

www.amberley-books.com

ISBN 978 1 4456 7238 0 (print)
ISBN 978 1 4456 7239 7 (ebook)

British Library Cataloguing in Publication Data.
A catalogue record for this book is available from the British Library.

Typeset in 10pt on 13pt Celeste.
Origination by Amberley Publishing.
Printed in the UK.

Contents

Acknowledgements

This book would not have been possible without the many people who have offered finds for recording with the Portable Antiquities Scheme – a project to record archaeological objects discovered by the public in England and Wales. Many of those finders are metal-detectorists, but they also include fieldwalkers and those who find 'portable antiquities' (archaeological small finds) completely by chance. By the same measure, I would also like to thank those that have identified and recorded these finds, especially the Finds Liaison Officers of the Portable Antiquities Scheme and its National Finds Advisers, but also the interns and volunteers, including those who have developed the necessary skills to record their own finds directly onto the Scheme's database (finds.org.uk/database). Many individuals have supported this book in a personal capacity. I would especially like to thank Rob Webley and the late David Williams, who have commented on the whole text, but also Megan von Ackermann, Kurt Adams, Jo Ahmet, Victoria Allnatt, Steven Ashley, Gary Bankhead, Frank Basford, Anna Booth, Andrew Brown, Laura Burnett, Anni Byard, Marian Campbell, Barrie Cook, Eleanore Cox, Adam Daubney, Teresa Gilmore, Rebecca Griffiths, Richard Henry, Katie Hinds, Duncan Hook, Amy Jeffs, Philippa Langley, Kevin Leahy, Sam Moorhead, Stuart Noon, Vanessa Oakden, Eljas Oksanen, Ben Paites, Tim Pestell, Ian Richardson, Corneliu Thira, Colin Torode, Ros Tyrrell and Edwin Wood. Apologies to anyone I have accidentally missed...

Preface

The Portable Antiquities Scheme is without doubt one of the most important innovations in British archaeology over the last twenty years. Before it existed, there was no mechanism for systematically recording archaeological finds made by the public, especially crucial since the rise in the popularity of metal-detecting. Metal-detecting can be damaging to archaeology, but if practised responsibly (as outlined in the Code of Practice for Responsible Metal Detecting in England and Wales) can make an enormous contribution to our understanding of the past. Detectorists mostly search on ploughed land (where archaeology is vulnerable to damage) and they also prospectively search in areas unlikely to be explored by archaeologists. This can bring to light new and important discoveries, as well as identify new types of finds and sites of archaeological interest. For the British Museum, the Portable Antiquities Scheme is a vitally important partnership project, where we, working with local partners across England and in cooperation with colleagues in Wales, contribute to local archaeology, as well as work with local communities to learn more about our shared past.

Dr Hartwig Fischer
Director of the British Museum

A metal-detecting survey on the site of the Battle of Barnet, 1471. (Author)

Introduction

The medieval period, taken here to be *c.* AD 1050 to *c.* AD 1550, is one of the most exciting periods of European history. As a medieval archaeologist and (sometime) historian I am certainly biased, but many (probably also medievalists) would not disagree!

It is somewhat artificial to divide the medieval era into neat sections of time, but there can be little doubt there is a notable distinction between the period from the decline of the Roman Empire (from about AD 400) to the mid-eleventh century – sometimes poorly described as the Dark Ages – and that from about 1050 until the Protestant Reformation of the mid-sixteenth century. Historians will divide time by notable events, of which the Norman Conquest of England was one of the most, if not the most, important to affect the British Isles, even though from the perspective of archaeological small finds (especially metallic ones) 1066 was a non-event!

Across Western Europe the period from 1050 to 1550 was archaeologically, and historically, important. It witnessed the beginnings of a period of transformation – a process which saw greater European unity, not necessarily in terms of political homogeny, but rather in terms of how humans understood the world around them, their appreciation of art and culture, and requirements of material culture (man-made materials). This is not to belittle the diversity that existed before, but it was increasingly the case that, through trade and the transmission of ideas, object-types used in England would have also been used in Italy, and styles found in Germany would be experienced in Spain. Europe (and its world) had become smaller.

Likewise, from the mid-sixteenth century, the end of our period, Europe witnessed seismic changes that radically altered the way people thought and behaved for centuries to come, ultimately influencing our way of life today. Generally considered as a religious event, the catalyst for Reformation of the 'old religion' was in fact the coming together of many factors, some cultural and some political. People across Europe became thirsty for greater knowledge than before, and through notable inventions, such as the printing press, had access to literary material (also available in the vernacular) that made them question the world order that had stood throughout the Middle Ages. This also led to a Renaissance in cultural thinking that transcended political and physical boundaries, particularly influencing art and literature.

In 1050 England was governed by a Christian king, Edward 'the Confessor', who both politically and culturally identified himself with monarchs in other parts of Europe. His kingship witnessed England turning its back on cultural ties with Scandinavia, notably Denmark, and instead looking towards Continental Europe: his mother, Emma, was Norman. Edward was known for welcoming foreigners and importing their ideas. During his reign the Romanesque style was first apparent in England, epitomised by his rebuilding of Westminster Abbey. 500 years later, England was still governed by a Christian king, another Edward – Edward VI. He was the first English king raised as a Protestant, and (through his officials) took forward the Reform of the English Church started by his father, Henry VIII. This period was to witness the greatest religious change this country saw since the conversion of the Anglo-Saxons to Christianity in the late sixth century. England in 1550 was therefore little like that of 1050, and subsequently the range of archaeological materials found by chance, by metal-detectorists and others, informs on that story of transformation and change.

It is often said that history books ignore the lives of everyday people in favour of those of great rulers, aristocrats and churchmen. Archaeology often does the opposite. It is certainly the case that the archaeological objects found by the public and recorded by the Portable Antiquities Scheme have interesting stories to tell, and sometimes help give a voice to people from the past otherwise forgotten by history. The objects presented here are not necessarily the most important medieval items recorded by the Scheme over the last twenty years, or even the most aesthetically pleasing. Instead, they have been chosen because of the stories they tell us about the past, and the extent to which they give a flavour of medieval life in England.

Nowadays, most people experience the Middle Ages through visiting churches and other buildings. Shown here are the remains of Castle Acre Priory, Norfolk, an important religious site that was suppressed, like many others in England, during the Reformation. (Author)

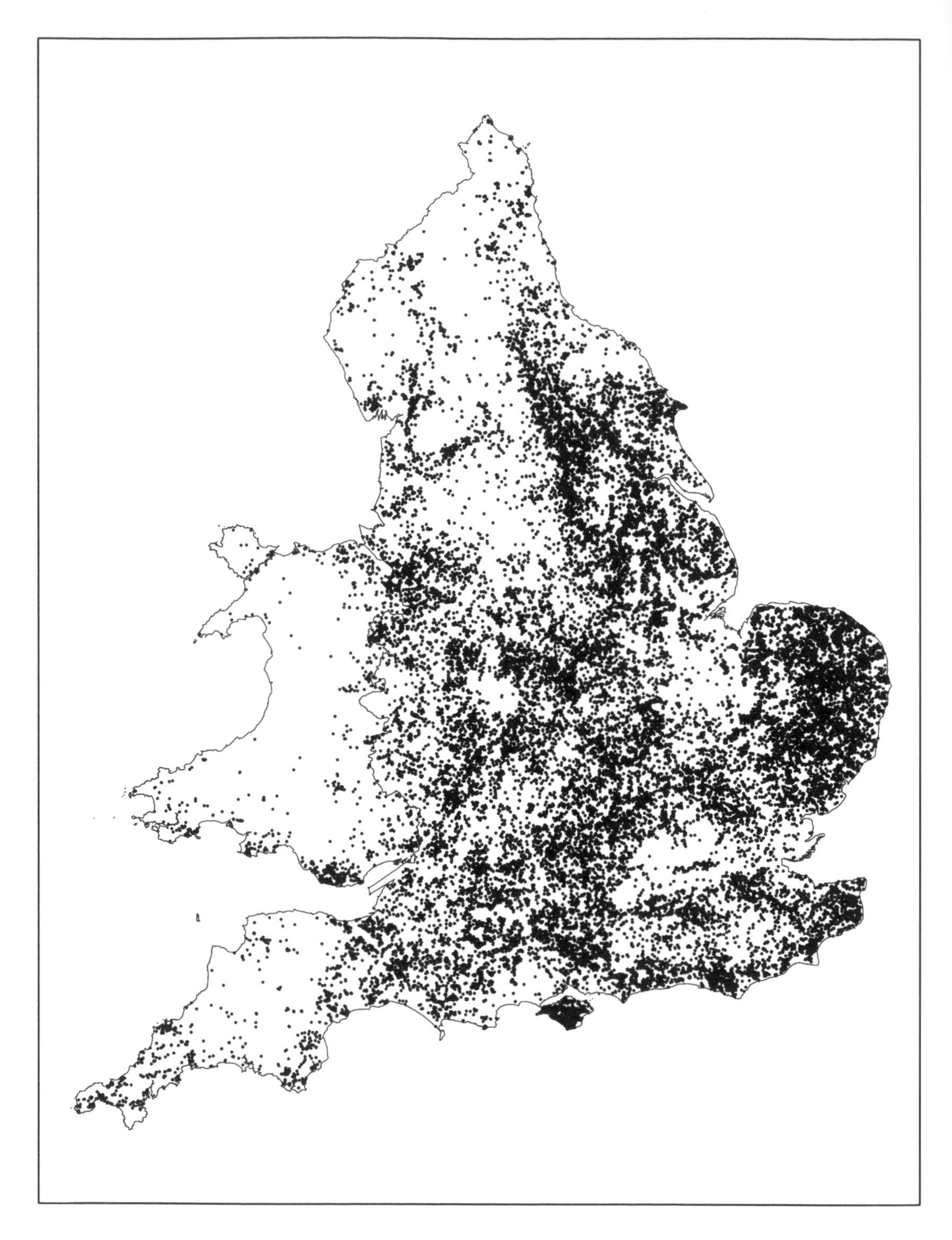

Map of medieval finds recorded with the PAS. (Eljas Oksanen)

Chapter 1
Kings and Knights

Medieval society was hierarchical, headed by the monarch (invariably a king) and his closest associates – predominately men of noble birth. Items known to be owned by these individuals are rare, and are unlikely to have been mislaid by chance: one notable exception is the royal treasure lost by King John in the Wash, which may remain to be discovered. However, now and again, objects are found that have royal or aristocratic connections, allowing us a rare, if not unique, opportunity to get close to those who ruled and governed medieval England.

A manuscript illustration of Richard II and his court. (British Library)

1. Hawking ring, silver, *c.* 1483, from Eaton Bray, Bedfordshire (WMID-1738A6). Dimensions 17.3 mm x 1.5 mm. Identified and recorded by Duncan Slarke, with James Robinson and Michael Lewis.

Medieval hawking rings (known as vervels or varvels) are excessively rare finds, this being the only medieval one reported as Treasure via the Portable Antiquities Scheme. This example is of particular interest since its inscription – 'Prince / Edward' in Gothic script – shows that it once belonged to a royal hawk. Vervels were tied to the leather jesses of hunting birds, and could be connected to a leash tied to a block or perch, ensuring the animal was grounded when not being flown. The inscriptions upon them (which are more informative in the post-medieval period) help identify the bird's owner, which was especially useful if hawks became lost, or were grouped together, such as on a hunt. There are numerous candidates for the Prince Edward mentioned on this vervel, but the most likely seems to be Edward, Prince of Wales, the future Edward V – one of the 'Princes in the Tower'. The findspot is also of great interest, since it is on the route Edward probably took, in April 1483 (following news of the death of his father, Edward IV), when he was intercepted by Richard, Duke of Gloucester (later Richard III) and escorted to London. Here he was taken to the Tower of London, ostensibly for his protection, but then vanished from history. It is a mystery what exactly happened to him, and his younger brother, Richard of Shrewsbury, but it is generally thought they were murdered: the main beneficiary being Richard III, who was crowned king two months later.

Hawking ring with the inscription 'Prince Edward', found at Eaton Bray, Bedfordshire. (PAS: WMID-1738A6)

Above: A hawk being flown. (Author)

Below right: Woodcut print of Edward V, and his brother, in the Tower of London. (British Museum)

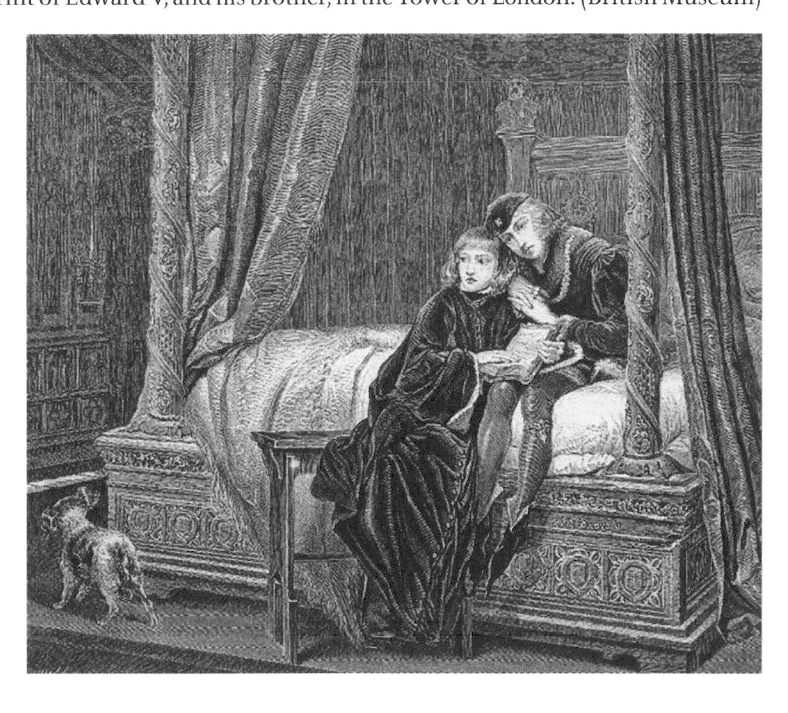

2. Quarter-florin of Edward III, gold, 1344, from Colyton, Devon (FASAM-638757).
Dimensions: 17 mm. Identified and recorded by Sam Moorhead.

Coinage was an important political tool, providing a means for the monarch to assert his identity and authority, but it also can reflect economic change. For many centuries the silver penny was the standard issue of coin produced in medieval England, but during Edward III's reign gold coinage was re-introduced; this was especially important on the international market, including for the wool trade with Flanders. Three new denominations were produced: the double leopard (equal to 6 shillings or 1 florin), leopard (3 shillings or half a florin) and helm (one and a half shillings or a quarter-florin). The coin shown here is an example of the latter, one of just a few known examples. The coinage was unsuccessful, not least because it over-valued gold in relation to silver, and it was therefore only issued from January to July 1344. By August it had been withdrawn from circulation, to be melted down in favour of producing gold nobles and derivative fractions which were more conveniently divisible by the mark and pound: both units of accounting. The obverse of this coin utilises aspects of Edward III's great seal of 1340, showing a helmet (hence its name), surmounted by a lion-like leopard, on a background of fleurs-de-lis, with the inscription EDWR R AnGL [Z FR]AnC D hIB (Edward, King of England and France, Lord of Ireland). The reverse depicts a floriated cross with a quatrefoil in its centre and the inscription EXALTABITVR In GLORIA (He shall be exalted in Glory, from Psalm 112:9). Edward III claimed the French throne through his mother, Isabella of France. This, therefore, is the first English coin to assert that claim, through the title 'King of France' and the use of fleur-de-lis (the symbol of France).

Helm or quarter-florin of Edward III, from Colyton, Devon. (PAS: FASAM-638757)

Above: Gold noble of Edward III, from Buckingham, West Sussex. (PAS: SUSS-4078FE)

Right: Engraving of Edward III. (British Museum)

3. Clasp frame, copper alloy, *c.* 1350 – *c.* 1400, from Ringwould, Kent (KENT-CF9AD8).
Dimensions: 37.9 mm x 19.2 mm x 6.5 mm. Identified and recorded by Jennifer Jackson.

Medieval kings believed they had a divine right to rule, and consequently could be ruthless and uncompromising. The royal image was a useful way to underline the authority of the king, and it is therefore of little surprise that images of the royal bust are found on everyday objects, such as this clasp frame. The king's portrait is shown very much like that on contemporary coinage, particularly the ubiquitous silver penny. It depicts the monarch facing forwards, his features clearly executed, and wearing a foliate crown with circular perforations. The frame is recessed (to take the plate) allowing it to function as a clasp, perhaps on a belt-strap or similar. Complete examples from excavations in London show that a rectangular plate was fixed to the frame's rounded bar; this would have been attached to a leather strap. Of a similar form are small mounts, probably used to complement the design of the folding clasp, which are likely to have been riveted to the leather strap.

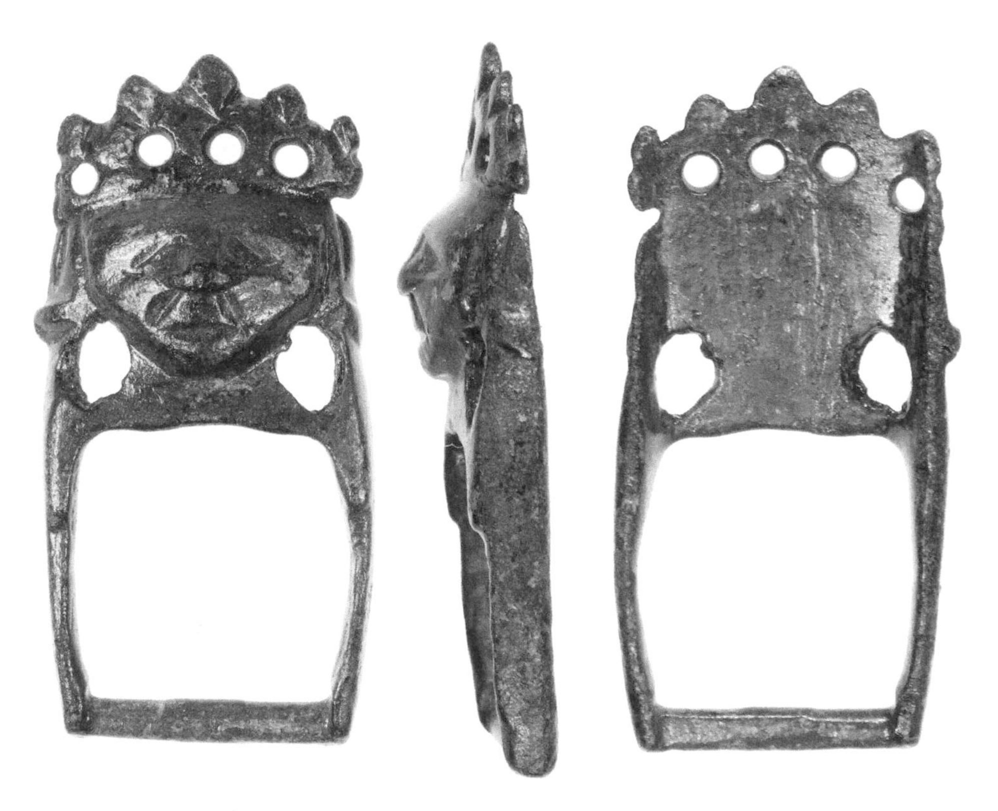

Clasp frame in the form of a king's head, from Ringwould, Kent. (PAS: KENT-CF9AD8)

The king's image on a silver penny of Edward III, from Keelby, Lincolnshire. (PAS: LIN-C8BC73)

Mount in the form of a king's head, from East Yorkshire. (PAS: YORYM-9CE553)

4. Penny of King John, silver, *c.* 1207–11, from Taynton, Gloucestershire (GLO-730921).
Dimensions: 19 mm x 0.7 mm. Identified and recorded by Kurt Adams.

In 1155, Pope Adrian IV granted King Henry II of England permission to invade Ireland, on the premise of curbing ecclesiastical corruption and abuses; Adrian IV (Nicholas Breakspear) was the only Englishman to be elected to the papacy. It was not until 1171, however, that Henry first landed in Ireland. The grant of Irish lands was ratified by Adrian's successor, Pope Alexander III, in 1172, with Henry then passing these to his younger son, John, on whom he conferred the title Lord of Ireland. Marking John's lordship over Ireland (but as king) is this silver penny. It shows the forward-facing bust of the king within a triangle, the motif used on Irish coins minted in the name of English monarchs, with the inscription IOhA/NNES/ REX (King John). The reverse has at its centre the sun, moon and three stars, also within a triangular frame. The legend on this side gives the name of the moneyer and the place the coin was minted: ROBE/RD ON/ DIVE (Robert in Dublin). The main purpose of John's Irish coinage was to drain the province of silver to support his unsuccessful campaigns against the French. It is not unusual for Irish pennies to be found in England, but their design is certainly special.

Penny of King John minted in Ireland, found at Taynton, Gloucestershire. (PAS: GLO-730921)

Penny of King John minted in London, found at Kilpin, East Yorkshire (PAS: LVPL-A0DA31). English pennies of John continue to use his father's name, Henry (II).

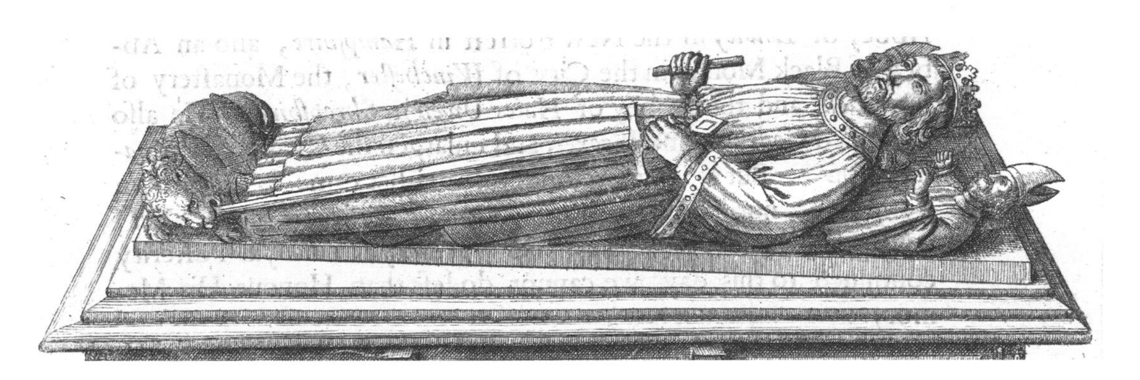

Drawing of King John's tomb in Worcester Cathedral. (British Museum)

5. Mount, copper alloy, *c.* 1460–85, from Tower Hamlets, London (LON-A33FF5).
Dimensions: 50.42 mm x 36.98 mm x 7.43 mm. Identified and recorded by Kate Sumnall.

During the Middle Ages it became popular for leading nobles, members of their household and supporters to wear livery badges, often as a mark of political allegiance. These might derive from the heraldic arms of such individuals, but could also develop independently, such as with a pun on the family name; John Talbot, the 1st Earl of Shrewsbury, for example, took for his badge the Talbot hunting-dog, though it is not apparent in his arms. This example from London is in the form of a boar, though it might be better described as a mount, as upon its reverse are three rivets, probably for fixing it to leather or possibly wood. It has been cast in the style of a heraldic crest with the animal facing right and standing on a twisted rope. The boar has a crown around its neck serving as a collar, and there is also a crescent marked on its shoulder. It is well known that Richard, Duke of Gloucester (1452–85), later Richard III, took the white boar for his personal emblem, though this example is presently coloured gold. It might be the case that the boar was adopted by Richard as a pun on the Roman name for York, Eboracum, contracted as Ebor, and white being the colour of the rose of the House of York during the Wars of the Roses: Richard was known as 'Richard of York' before being made Duke of Gloucester in 1461. Boar badges were ordered for use at Richard's coronation in July 1483, and the investiture of his young son, Edward, as Prince of Wales, the following September. A silver boar badge was also found at the site of the Battle of Bosworth, where Richard III was killed (LEIC-A6C834).

'The wretched, bloody, and usurping boar, that spoiled your summer fields and fruitful vines, swills your warm blood like wash, and makes his trough in your embowelled bosoms – this foul swine is now even in the centre of this isle, near to the town of Leicester, as we learn', Henry, Earl of Richmond, talking about Richard III (William Shakespeare, *Richard III,* Act 5, Scene 2).

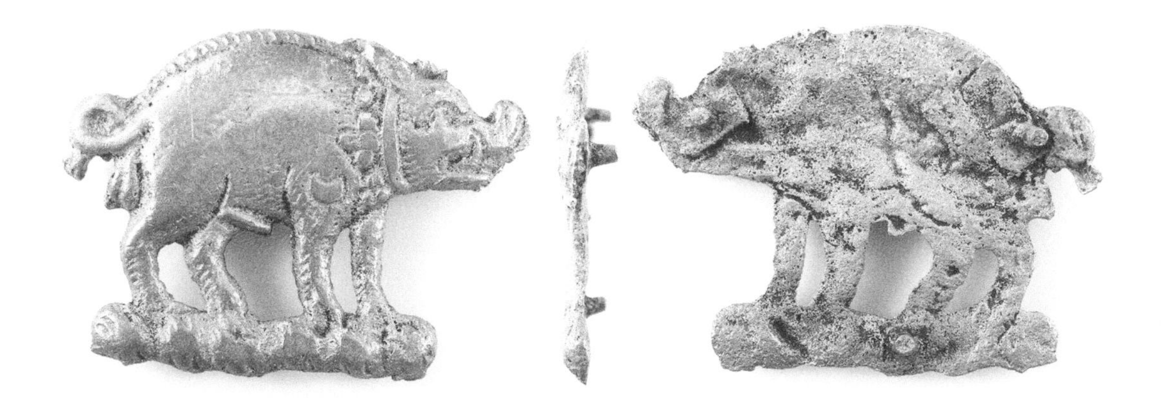

Boar mount from Tower Hamlets, London. (PAS: LON-A33FF5)

Banner of Richard III. (Courtesy of the Richard III Society)

Richard III's tomb. (Author)

6. Heraldic mount, copper alloy, *c.* 1250 – *c.* 1400, from Datchworth, Hertfordshire (BH-1AA2D3).
Dimensions: 64.5 mm x 46.9 mm x 2 mm. Identified and recorded by Julian Watters, with Steven Ashley.

The knight was an important figure in the Middle Ages, ensuring kings remained strong and their kingdoms secure. This mount takes the form of a fully armed knight on horseback, galloping left. The figure wears a helmet, of great helm type. His right arm is held backwards, with the forearm bent upwards from the elbow, and the hand gripping the hilt of a sword, the point of which rests on top of the helmet. The knight's body is obscured by an angled shield, the position of which suggests it is held in the left hand. Upon the shield are three silver crosses on a red background divided by a silver zigzag band, described in heraldic language as *Gules a fess dancetty Argent between three crosses formy Argent*. These arms also appear on the horse's trapper, and might be those of the Longville family (*Gules crusily a fess dancetty Argent*), who held manors in Northamptonshire and Huntingdonshire in about 1300. Much of the red enamelling survives in recessed fields on the mount, though the raised parts of the design (which were once silver) have now tarnished black. The mount has five rivet holes, of which the copper-alloy rivets survive in two. It is not known what the object was once attached to, though it might be that it was for display on a furnishing, such as a chest or casket.

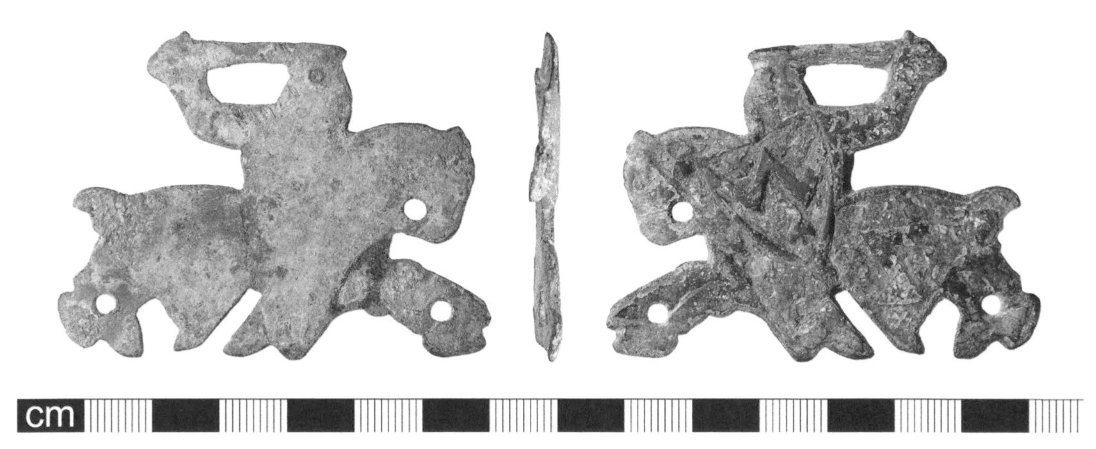

Heraldic mount from Datchworth, Hertfordshire. (PAS: BH-1AA2D3)

Re-enactor, showing the medieval knight in all his finery. (Author)

7. Seal matrix, copper alloy, *c.* 1200–58, from Little Bedwyn, Wiltshire (BERK-FDCFD2).
Dimensions: 54.18 mm x 12.75 mm x 7.3 mm. Identified and recorded by Anni Byard, with Adrian Ailes, John Cherry and Clive Cheesman.

Matrices, such as this, were used to make wax seals for use on vellum documents. Numerous examples have been recorded through the Portable Antiquities Scheme, and were used by people of various social echelons. One of the most distinguished recorded in recent years is this seal matrix of Fulk III FitzWarin, Lord of Whittington, Shropshire. This object, of which a large section of the lower part is missing, shows Fulk in full armour, mounted, and surrounded by the legend SIGILLVM F[VLCONIS FIL]II WARINI (seal of Fulk FitzWarin). The seal image is incredibly well defined, so that the knight's mail, the folds in his surcoat, and the horse's harness equipment, including harness pendants, are clear to see. Upon the knight's shield is emblazoned the FitzWarin arms: *quarterly per fess indented agent and gules* (divided quarterly with a fess indented, the opposite quarters coloured silver and red). Unlike many matrices recorded with the Portable Antiquities Scheme, which were only used to stamp a design onto the wax surface, this is the obverse of a two-part matrix for making a double-sided wax seal. It has pin at the top, which would have been matched by another on the missing part, ensuring that the two matrices (obverse and reverse) could be aligned. Fulk III was an important marcher lord who rebelled against King John and was subsequently outlawed; he appears in the medieval romance *Fouke le Fitz Waryn,* which might have inspired parts of the legend of Robin Hood. In July 1202, Fulk and his followers took refuge at Stanley Abbey, near Studley, Wiltshire, which is only 20 miles to the east of the findspot, near the thirteenth-century Chisbury Chapel. It is perhaps at this time that the seal matrix was lost. The following year Fulk was pardoned, having his lands returned. He also seems to have benefited from incredible longevity, as it is claimed he was ninety-eight years old when he died.

Seal of Fulk III FitzWarin from Little Bedwyn, Wiltshire. (PAS: BERK-FDCFD2)

8. Harness pendant, copper alloy, *c.* 1321–77, from Melbourn, Cambridgeshire (BH-3FF1E6).
Dimensions: 41.5 mm x 27.9 mm x 6.9 mm. Identified and recorded by Julian Watters, with Steven Ashley.

Heraldic pendants are relatively common finds, and were used to decorate horse harnesses in the Middle Ages. Their form varies considerably, although lozengiform examples are less frequently found than the majority, which are shield-shaped (see page 24). The arms on this pendant are of special interest since they quarter two important families, joined together in matrimony – Aylmer de Valence, the 2nd Earl of Pembroke and Montgomery, and Marie de St Pol, née Châtillon. This treatment reflects the fact that Marie had status in her own right, and her pedigree was important to her husband. The first and fourth quarters show a field of silver and blue horizontal bars, with three red martlets (a bird similar to a house martin or swallow) on top; the martlets are normally shown as a border of eight (*barry of ten Argent and Azure over all eight martlets in orle Gules*). The second and third quarters have vertical bands of red and vair (squirrel fur), with a gold band across the top, and upon it a blue label of three points (*Gules and Vair on a chief Or a label of three points Azure*). The arms, though normally shown halved (impaled), not quartered, are also borne by Pembroke College, Cambridge, which Marie founded in 1321. The pendant's suspension loop shows little sign of wear, so it is possible that the object was lost not long after it was made. It is likely that the object dates from between 1321, when the couple were married, and Marie's death, in 1377.

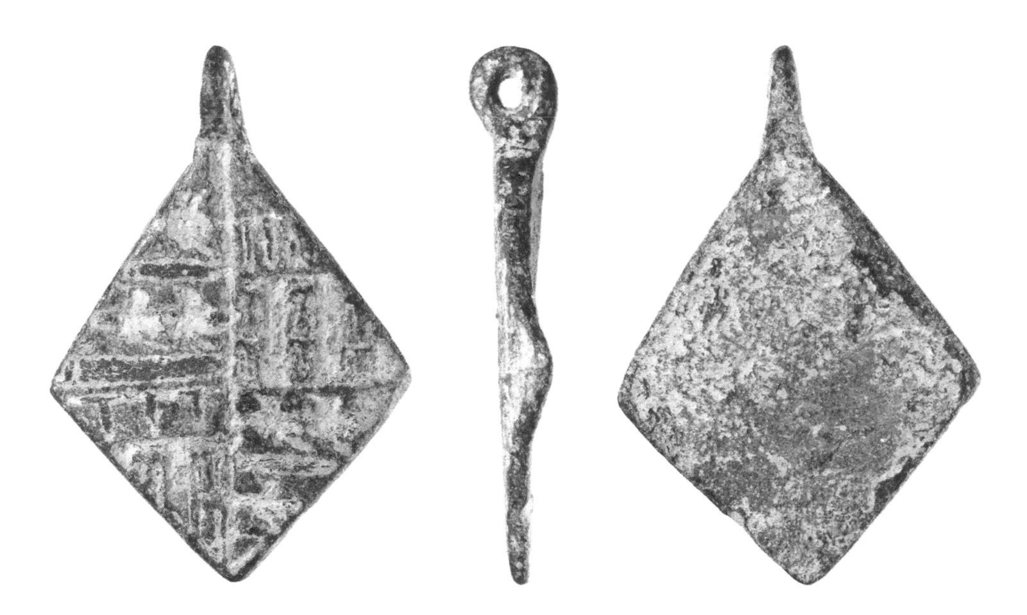

Harness pendant of Aylmer de Valence and Marie de St Pol, from Melbourn, Cambridgeshire. (PAS: BH-3FF1E6)

Above: Pembroke College, Cambridge. (Author)

Left: Harness pendant from Clanfield, Oxfordshire. (PAS: BH-33092C)

9. Crossbow bolt, iron, *c.* 1300 – *c.* 1400, from the City of London (LON-CEFFCD). Dimensions: 47.91 mm x 12.52 mm x 7.81 mm. Identified and recorded by Edwin Wood, with Sharon Sullivan.

Iron finds from the Middle Ages are not common as detector finds, especially since the metal does not preserve well in most soil conditions. It is also the case that most metal-detector users set their machines to discriminate against finding it since most iron finds turn out to be modern. The discovery of this arrowhead is therefore somewhat remarkable, especially as it has within it the remains of its wooden shaft. It survives thanks to the anaerobic conditions of the river-mud of the Thames foreshore in which it was found. The object is short, with a diamond cross-section point, and circular socket. Its point is barbed, though these protrusions are narrow and short. The arrowhead is of military type, for use in a crossbow, as opposed to being used for hunting. Sometimes known as a 'short bodkin', this arrow type developed in response to the advancement of plate armour that, from about the middle of the fourteenth century, was increasingly popular on the Continent, although such arrows would only be particularly dangerous to the fully armoured knight at close range. That said, plated armour was prohibitively expensive for all but the elite, and therefore most soldiers on the medieval battlefield would have been extremely vulnerable to such projectiles.

Crossbow bolt from the City of London. (PAS: LON-CEFFCD)

Above: Medieval manuscript showing both the use of the longbow and crossbow. (British Library)

Left: Re-enactor firing an arrow from a longbow. (Author)

10. Sword, iron, *c.* 1100 – *c.* 1200, from Bury St Edmunds area, Suffolk (SF-9EF0BA).
Dimensions: 940.20 mm x 150.4 mm x 60.5 mm. Identified and recorded by Anna Booth, with Edward Martin and Beverley Nenk. Acquired by Moyse's Hall Museum, Bury St Edmunds.

The weapon par excellence of the medieval knight was his sword. During the early medieval period pattern-welded weapons were highly prized, due to the skill and time needed to produce their blades: rods of iron were twisted together and then hammered flat, giving the blade both strength and its attractive pattern. The swordsmith, like the wordsmith, was much respected and admired at this time, both traditions giving rise to a belief in the magical properties of swords, as wielded by heroes of legend, such as Beowulf. Although by the high Middle Ages swords were more commonly owned, it was still the case that quality weapons could only be afforded by the elite. This sword, of relatively early date, is extremely well preserved given it is substantially made of iron. Besides the blade, also surviving is its hilt, complete with cross-guard and 'brazil nut'-shaped pommel. Also found with the sword was the remains of its leather sheath. The sword blade has upon it an inscription, made with silver wire inlay, reading + DEANDVHEFNDTHENMDAEHRAEH + (the A's are all upside-down and the last two H's have double crossbars), the meaning of which is unclear. At the hilt-end of the blade is a decorative motif consisting of (probable) birds with a plume or feather. Silver inlaid inscriptions are known on other swords of this date, which are often religious. It has been suggested that this sword, which was found within waterlogged material in a pond, might have been lost during a local skirmish in about 1173/74.

Sword with inscription from Bury St Edmunds area, Suffolk. (PAS: SF-9EF0BA)

X-ray of the sword's inscription. (PAS: SF-9EF0BA)

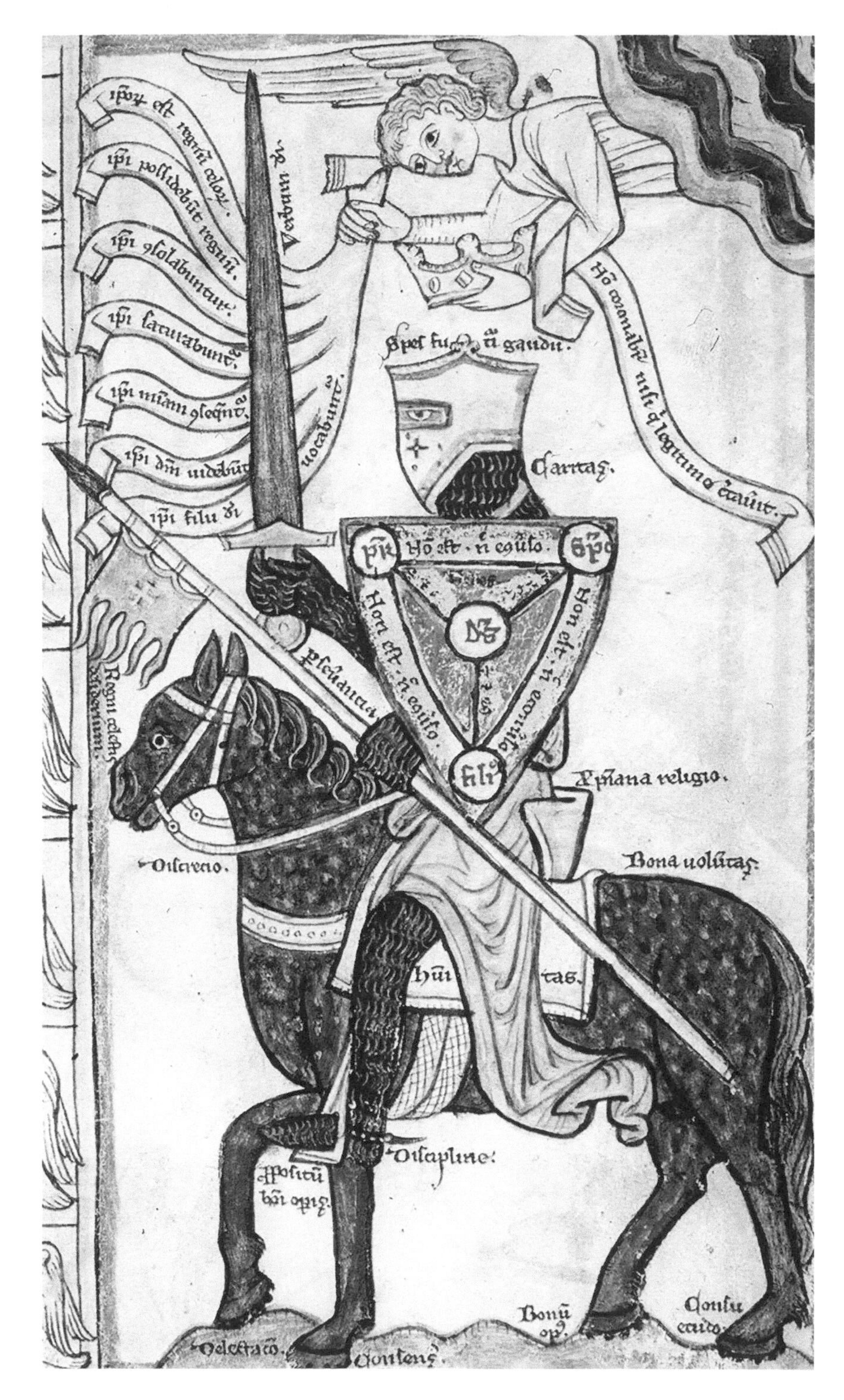

Knight with a sword in a medieval manuscript. (British Library)

Chapter 2
Dress and Jewellery

Fashion was an important part of life in the Middle Ages, although only the extremely well-off could afford dress and jewellery made from the finest materials, often produced in gaudy colours. Few textiles survive from this period, so what we know of medieval dress comes from contemporary depictions, which are more numerous than might be expected; they include a memorial brass cited here. Much more common are finds of dress accessories, some precious metal, but many more of base metals and therefore likely to have been worn by those of lesser social importance. It is therefore the case that the finds recorded with the Portable Antiquities Scheme provide insights into fashions of the population at large, not just the elite.

Three women, in costly garments, being taught how to read in a medieval manuscript. (British Library)

11. Finger-ring, gold with gemstones, *c.* 1175 – *c.* 1225, from Hursley, Hampshire (HAMP-0B7C35).
Dimensions: 24 mm x 22.6 mm. Identified and recorded by Katie Hinds, with John Cherry. Acquired by Hampshire Cultural Trust (Winchester collections).

Medieval finger-rings were made in a great variety of forms and styles, and were worn by both men and women. Particularly impressive and sophisticated is this gold finger-ring set with three stones. It has a central oval bezel set with a cabochon setting; this colourless stone has been identified through Raman spectroscopy as corundum (sapphire). The shoulders of the ring have plain bands, and are also set either side of the central bezel with two smaller horizontal red cabochon stones, in oval settings, flanked by raised ridges; these stones are almandine garnets. During the Middle Ages there was a popular belief in the inherent powers of gems, both for their medicinal and quasi-magical properties, also making them collectable.

Gold finger-ring with gemstones, from Hursley, Hampshire. (PAS: HAMP-0B7C35)

Right: Late medieval base-metal finger-ring, from Lambeth, London. (PAS: LON-DD4125)

Below: The giving of a finger-ring, as shown in a medieval manuscript. (British Library)

12. Iconographic finger-ring, gold, *c.* 1400 – *c.* 1500, from Bruton, Somerset (SOM-5D3915).
Dimensions: 20.3 mm x 5.7 mm x 1.9 mm. Identified and recorded by Laura Burnett.

Iconographic finger-rings provide an important insight into personal devotion in the Middle Ages. Although representations of the Virgin Mary are common, also shown are a variety of important saints, in this case St James 'the Great'. Here he is shown, engraved in shallow relief, wearing a robe with a collar. The saint is bearded and haloed, and holds a scallop shell in his draped left hand. His right hand is raised, as if to indicate the shell in the other. The scallop shell was to become the symbol of St James, and is associated with both pilgrimage to his shrine at Santiago de Compostella in Spain and pilgrimage more generally. The hoop of the ring tapers evenly in width from the bezel and is decorated. Nearest the bezel can be seen deeply indented curved lines, which serve as rays of light from above and below the saint. On each side of the hoop are images of two indented flowers, all with five-petalled heads, and leaves on their stems. It is perhaps the case that the engraved areas were once enamelled, but if so nothing remains. Such objects were important devotional aids, helping medieval people focus on prayer, and the good works and sufferings of holy people.

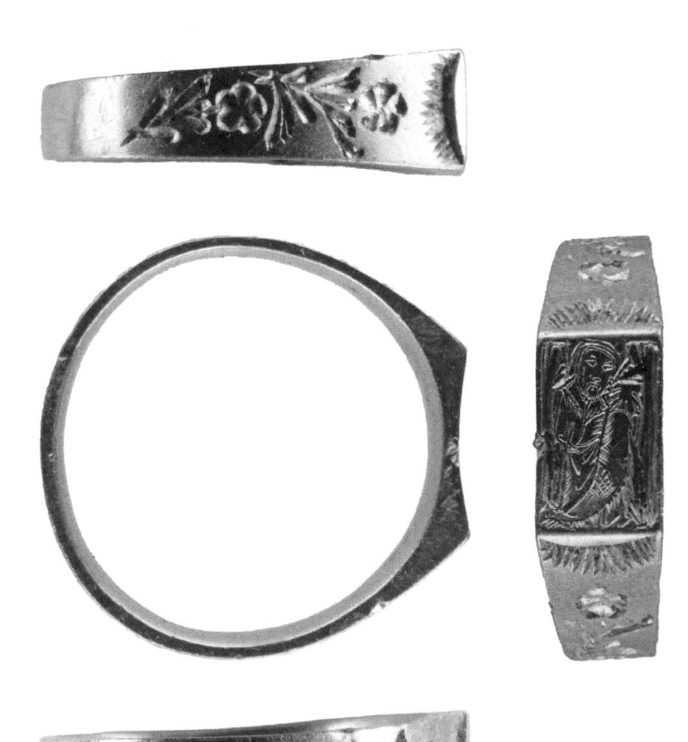

Gold iconographic finger-ring, from Bruton, Somerset. (PAS: SOM-5D3915)

Painting of St James on a medieval rood-screen. (Author)

13. Brooch made from a finger-ring, silver with gemstone, *c.* 1200 – *c.* 1400, from Newmarket area, Suffolk (CAM-B7D4E3).
Dimensions: 25.4 mm x 21.8 mm. Identified and recorded by Helen Fowler.

Stirrup-shaped finger-rings are a popular medieval type, but this example is particularly unusual since it has been repurposed as a brooch. Why this might have happened is uncertain, but maybe the ring no longer fitted the wearer or it was gifted to another; perhaps the original owner died and it was kept by a loved one. The ring has a sub-circular hoop with an internal width diameter of 18.5 mm, so it is most likely to have originally been worn by a woman, though this is not certain as both sexes wore quite ornate rings. A faint line can be seen at the base of the hoop on both sides, which shows that it was formed by its terminals being shaped to taper across opposing diagonal surfaces. These have been butted against each other tightly, and then worked to form a smooth continuous hoop so it has an almost perfect circular cross-section at the join; it is not known whether any adhesive, such as solder, was used to help hold the join. The hoop expands upwards to form a triangular zone that acts as a bezel to take a rosy-pink stone. The pin of the brooch, also of medieval date, is finely made. It tapers to a point, and has a decorative collar embellished with incised grooves.

Brooch made from a finger-ring, found near Newmarket, Cambridgeshire. (PAS: CAM-B7D4E3)

Stirrup-shaped finger-ring from Burgh St Peter, Norfolk. (PAS: NMS-8EADF3)

Brooch made from a short-cross penny, from Winteringham, North Lincolnshire. (PAS: DUR-A20215)

14. Brooch with inscription, gold, *c.* 1400 – *c.* 1500, from Arreton, Isle of Wight (IOW-506491).
Dimensions: 19.03 mm x 3.47 mm. Identified and recorded by Frank Basford and Beverley Nenk. Acquired by the British Museum.

This gold brooch is notably chunky, especially when compared with other annular brooches of the medieval period. Upon the display-side, the circular frame has been divided into chevrons. The inner ones, which are all evenly spaced, are decorated with cross-hatching so as to form a star. Those on the outside have in all but one instance a letter in Gothic script, the other has a cinquefoil; most of the letters have trefoils either side. When read together the letters say 'bien va' for 'go well' or 'be well'. This is probably an amatory legend, perhaps suggesting the brooch might have been a love gift. The pin survives intact, and still works, but is quite plain. The object clearly belonged to someone of status, especially given its quality and composition, though a number of inscribed base metal brooches have also been recorded with the Portable Antiquities Scheme.

Left: Gold brooch with inscription, from Arreton, Isle of Wight. (PAS: IOW-506491)

Right: Example of a base-metal brooch with inscription, found at Wotton, Surrey. (PAS: SUR-690FCC)

15. Brooch, silver-gilt with semi-precious stones, *c.* 1200 – *c.* 1300, from Raunds, Northamptonshire (NARC-1C626A).
Dimensions: 16.98 mm x 16.95 mm x 3.47 mm. Identified and recorded by Eleanore Cox.

Precious metal dress accessories, such as this brooch, would have been owned by the elite; its loss would have been noticed and missed. Brooches of similar form, but made of base-metal, show that those with less disposable income aspired to own such objects as well. This is an annular brooch with a quatrefoil openwork frame. At the junction of each quatrefoil is a projecting collet, each holding a single oval purple-red stone; these are possibly amethysts, a popular stone in the Middle Ages. An interesting aspect of this brooch is that only its frame is gilded. Its pin is silver and is formed of a single piece of tapering metal, of which the broadest end wraps around the brooch frame.

Left: Brooch with semi-precious stones, from Raunds, Northamptonshire. (PAS: NARC-1C626A)

Right: Quatrefoil openwork brooch, from Burton on the Wolds, Leicestershire. (PAS: LEIC-E477DB)

16. Buckle frame, gilded copper alloy, *c.* 1200, from Soham, Cambridgeshire (NMS-372328).
Dimensions: 33 mm x 26 mm. Identified and recorded by Steven Ashley, with Sandy Heslop.

This remarkable openwork buckle frame is a fantastic example of medieval craftsmanship. Sadly, it is not complete; both sides of the frame, the pin and probable plate are missing. The design is of two male seated figures wearing classically inspired robes. They have their heads slightly inclined towards one another, as if in conversation. Both of their faces are worn, as are other exposed elements, showing the object to be much used before its loss. Between the figures is a vertical curling lobed plant-like motif, the remains of which also survive as stumps on the outside edges of the buckle-frame. The object parallels a complete silver gilt example in the Dune Hoard, from Gotland, Sweden, which is now in the Statens Historiska Museum, Stockholm. Both are likely to be of English manufacture. Clearly then, this object is not typical of the buckles worn in the Middle Ages, of which the vast majority are less ornate, and mostly purely functional.

Buckle-frame showing two male figures, from Soham, Cambridgeshire. (PAS: NMS-372328)

This buckle from Costessey, Norfolk (NMS-F737B3) is typical of thirteenth-century buckles recorded with the Portable Antiquities Scheme (PAS).

17. Buckle, bone, *c.* 1100 – *c.* 1200, from Tower Hamlets, London (LON-FE5446). Dimensions: 32.96 mm x 25.19 mm x 7.12 mm. Identified and recorded by Kate Sunmall. Acquired by the Museum of London.

Although most of the buckles recorded with the Portable Antiquities Scheme are made of copper alloy, it must have been the case that many medieval dress accessories were made of worked bone or ivory, as well as other materials. Such items are rare survivals, this buckle of bone being preserved by the Thames mud until its discovery. The frame is D-shaped, and has been carved in one piece with the buckle plate: it has a notched pin-rest and is decorated with diagonal carved grooves. The pin pivots on a dowel inserted into the side of the buckle, which is visible only on one side. A similar buckle made of ivory was found during excavations at Jedburgh Abbey, Scottish Borders, Scotland, and a bone example was found at the deserted medieval village of Goltho, Lincolnshire.

Bone buckle from Tower Hamlets, London. (PAS: LON-FE5446)

D-shaped buckle from Nether Poppleton, North Yorkshire (DUR-59E9B3). Most buckles found by metal-detectorists are made of copper alloy, like this example (PAS).

18. Strap-end, copper alloy, *c.* 1400 – *c.* 1500, from Sutton, West Sussex (HAMP-A7E5D1).
Dimensions: 81.2 mm x 35.5 mm x 4.2 mm. Identified and recorded by Rob Webley, with James Robinson.

Leather and textile belts and straps were commonly worn in the Middle Ages, perhaps more so than today. When wearing a belt it was usual that the end of the strap fell loose, and therefore it needed some protection from accidental damage and wear, hence the purpose of a strap-end. Strap-ends varied considerably in form and design and the materials from which they were made. Most of those recorded by the Portable Antiquities Scheme are copper alloy, such as this rather splendid example. This high-status object is of elaborate construction, formed of four main elements: two sheet plates that have a rectangular body with expanding circular base, a spacer between them, and a plate for the display side showing a kneeling male figure in prayer within a niche, with a fleur-de-lis above. At the attachment end, where the strap-end would have joined the strap using rivets through the holes, there is a trifoliate aperture for decorative effect. Besides the additional plate with the figure upon it, the whole display-side is embellished with incised decoration, including both finely executed cross-hatching and geometric floral motifs. At the base of the object is a zoomorphic terminal. The posture of the figure has been likened to that of donors in religious art and on ecclesiastical seal matrices, so perhaps this strap-end might have belonged to a cleric. That said, the apparent religious nature of the object would have had a much wider appeal in the Middle Ages.

Strap-end from Sutton, West Sussex. (PAS: HAMP-A7E5D1)

Strap-end of a common type, from Shorwell, Isle of Wight. (PAS: IOW-931AE6)

Strap-end of a simple type, but with a decorative terminal, from Thornton, Buckinghamshire. (PAS: BUC-88E53B)

19. Mirror, copper alloy, *c.* 1150 – *c.* 1450, from Silchester, Hampshire (WILT-3CA276).
Dimensions: 43.95 mm x 31.45 mm x 9.85 mm (when closed). Identified and recorded by Richard Henry.

Nowadays we are used to seeing our own image, normally as a reflection or in a photograph or on a digital device, but this was not commonly the case in the Middle Ages. Nonetheless, finds of mirror cases show that medieval people had concern for their personal appearance. It is likely that such objects were made for women, and may have been given as love gifts. Gifting such items might have had sexual connotations, since a mirror (like the hopeful gift-giver) would see the lady, up close, in her bedchamber. Surviving from the medieval period are some impressive ivory mirror cases, beautifully carved with scenes of courtly romance, which were clearly made for the very rich. Recorded with the Portable Antiquities Scheme are less ornate examples, of which there are two main types produced in copper alloy. Some are decorated with glass squares, of which only the solder survives, and small collets, that once held stones. More common are those with incised decoration, of cruciform style. For both types, the mirror case is made of two identical halves, consisting of two circular flat-bottomed dishes with integrally cast fittings protruding from opposite sides. On one side, the fittings are riveted together and used as a hinge, and on the other, as a clasp, probably being kept shut with wire or string. In some instances, these mirror cases contain the tin-backed glass mirror itself, or just the white paste that served as cement to hold the mirror in place.

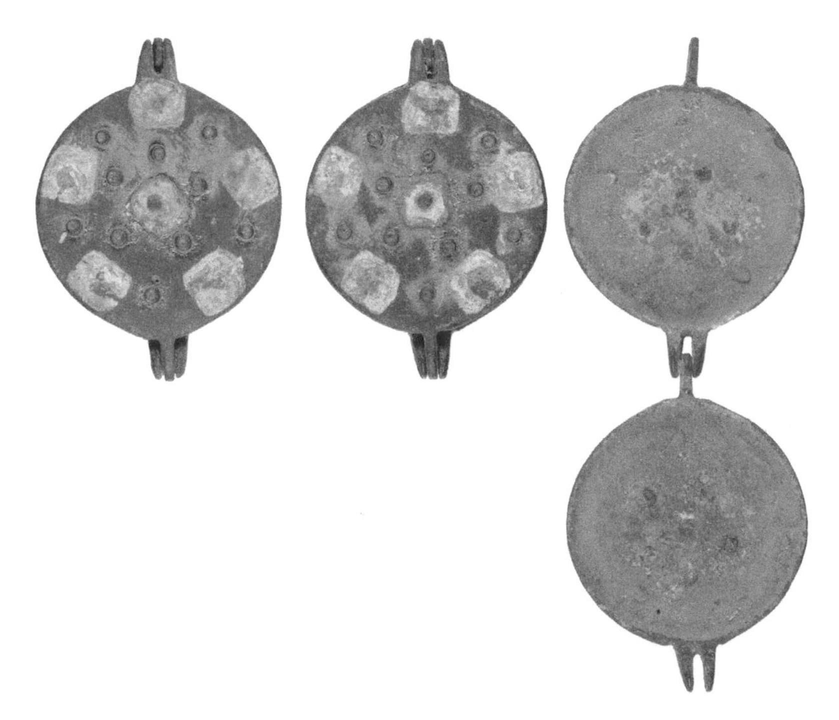

Mirror case with collets for stones, from Silchester, Hampshire. (PAS: WILT-3CA276)

Right: Mirror case with cruciform decoration, from Broad Hinton, Wiltshire. (PAS: WILT-BC14E5)

Below: Ivory mirror case. (Walters Art Museum/ Wikimedia Commons)

20. Memorial, copper alloy, *c.* 1520–50, from Keyham, Leicestershire (FAKL-31AF67).
Dimensions: 64 mm x 63 mm x 3 mm. Identified and recorded by Kevin Leahy.

Although this object dates towards the end of the medieval period, in the decades just before the Protestant Reformation, it provides good evidence for the type of dress worn at the time. It is a memorial brass fragment, showing two standing female figures, their hands clasped in prayer. Both wear 'kennel-shaped' headdresses, and outer garments with square-cut collars. Between the two women is a hole for fixing the plate to a church floor. The decoration on the back of the object suggests it has been made from an earlier monument, showing recycling is not new! Such memorials were important in the Middle Ages since they ensured the dead were prayed for, therefore enabling them a smoother path through purgatory to heaven (also see 30). In this case the two individuals are looking to the side, showing that they were not the principal figures on the brass, but they are probably children of the deceased, looking towards their dead mother or father, and praying for their soul.

Memorial from Keyham, Leicestershire. (PAS: FAKL-31AF67)

Medieval manuscript illustration showing Margaret of York in a very fine dress. (British Library)

Chapter 3
Church and Religion

Religion was a fundamental part of medieval life, with almost all the population being Christian; at times during the Middle Ages Jews were tolerated in England, especially as they had an essential role as money-lenders. At the head of the Church was the Pope, with the papal curia, instructing the life of all people through edicts, as well as granting indulgences. People were mostly devout, believing that they would be held to account for their actions on earth in the afterlife, and that they also had a duty to pray for the dead. Their piety and religious devotion can be seen in many of the objects recorded through the Portable Antiquities Scheme.

Lincoln Cathedral. The medieval cathedral dominates the modern town. (Author)

21. Papal bulla, lead, 1464–71, from Cheddon Fitzpaine, Somerset (SOM-FBA501).
Dimensions: 41.6 mm x 38.7 mm x 6.3 mm. Identified and recorded by Rob Webley.

Highlighting the influence of the papal curia across Christendom are documents in archives known as bulls or bullae, which often have upon them lead seals, also (and somewhat confusingly) known as bullae. These lead seals are relatively common metal-detector finds. Substantial numbers of them recorded with the Portable Antiquities Scheme date to the thirteenth century, showing the papacy being particularly active at this time. Usually one side (the obverse) gives the name of the Pope in whose name the seal was issued, while the other (the reverse) shows the busts of St Paul and St Peter, with their names abbreviated as SPA SPE above. These bullae hung from the documents to which they were attached with a silk or hemp cord, which rarely survives. An unusual example in regards to its design is this papal bulla issued in the name of Paul II (Pietro Barbo, r. 1464–71), one-time Venetian merchant, who was the only Pope to have his matrices significantly redesigned. The reverse shows St Peter and St Paul enthroned each side of an orb, with their abbreviated names above. The obverse has the Pope enthroned, flanked by a cardinal on either side, and (to the right) his flock kneeling in prayer. Above this scene is the legend PAVLVS. / PP. II: 'PP' stands for Pastor Pastorum (shepherd of the shepherds). The fact that Paul II is shown flanked by cardinals is somewhat ironic, for his papacy was marred by his abuse of the practice of creating supporters as cardinals without publishing their names. Prior to his election Pietro Barbo even boasted that if he became Pope he would buy each cardinal a summer villa, to escape Rome's heat! After his papacy, seals reverted to their traditional form.

Lead bulla of Pope Paul II. (PAS: SOM-FBA501)

Lead bulla of Pope Boniface IX, found at Cothelstone, Somerset (SOM-C31329), showing the design of bullae used by most popes (PAS).

This papal bulla, found near Caerleon, Newport, is broken in half, revealing the fibres of its suspension cord. (PAS: NMGW-47FD0C)

22. Mount, copper alloy, *c.* 1100 – *c.* 1250, from Milverton, Somerset (SOM-3E316A).
Dimensions: 33.9 mm x 18.4 mm x 10.9 mm. Identified and recorded by Laura Burnett, with Marian Campbell and Rob Webley.

Previously attached to a vessel, casket or (perhaps) staff is this highly decorative gilded copper-alloy finial; the integral rivet at its base shows that it was attached to a larger object. It is in the form of a bird of prey, probably an eagle, grasping with its claws a quadruped, suggested to be a dog or lion. The object is finely moulded, with details, such as the bird's wings, folded onto its back with the tips crossed, picked out with incised lines. Gilding, though worn, is present on the most visible parts of the object, excluding its underneath and the base. The bird has inlaid circular glass eyes that are a bright blue-green; one is battered, the other cracked. The subdued beast has its eyes covered by the raptor's left-footed grasp, its tail between its legs, though it is still standing. The art style of the object appears to be Romanesque, suggested by the form of the animal, the finery of the metal-working, and use of glass inlay for its eyes. Its use in England is evident from the middle of the eleventh century, though is often associated with the Anglo-Norman period. English artists contributed greatly to the Romanesque style, highlighted by fine examples of illuminated manuscripts, as well as architecture and stone sculpture. To date, exact parallels for this mount have not yet been identified, marking its significance.

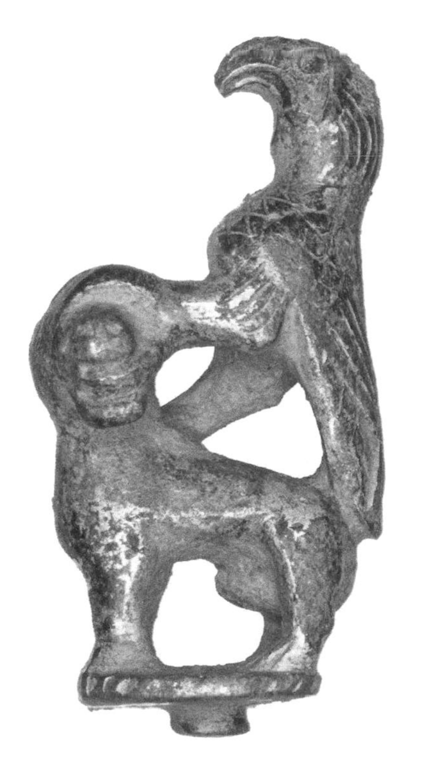

Romanesque mount from Milverton, Somerset. (PAS: SOM-3E316A)

Hunting bird in the Bayeux Tapestry. (Author)

Anglo-Norman stirrup-strap mount from Cheriton, Hampshire showing a Romanesque beast. (PAS: HAMP-9DA925)

23. Mount, gilded copper alloy, *c.* 1170 – *c.* 1300, from Therfield, Hertfordshire (BH-0D0F26).
Dimensions: 50.3 mm x 36.7 mm x 1.4 mm. Identified and recorded by Julian Watters.

These T-shaped mounts were applied to the back of processional and altar crosses, and appear to have been relatively common in the Middle Ages. They normally show a stylised representation of one of the four Evangelists (authors of the Gospels), this being the Ox of St Luke, a convention applied to enable the illiterate to 'read' visual narratives common in pre-Reform churches. This mount is of a form known to have been produced at the important enamelling workshops of Limoges, France. Once this object would have been decorated in the recessed areas with brightly coloured enamels, typical of Limoges-work, where the colours bleed into one another, such as on a poppy or pansy. On this example only a small amount of dark blue enamelling survives. The raised areas were commonly gilded, which is the case on this mount, although little remains. In the corners of the mount are rivet holes, which would have enabled it to be fixed to a wooden cross, the complete object being covered with such enamels, hiding the wooden structure beneath. On the reverse of the mount is the unusual feature of a small arrow, pointing downwards, presumed to have been an aid to positioning the mount onto the cross. It is likely that such Limoges enamels entered the ground during the English Reformation of the mid-sixteenth century, when many non-precious church objects considered to be idolatrous were broken up or destroyed since they had little intrinsic value.

Limoges mount from a processional cross, from Therfield, Hertfordshire. (PAS: BH-0D0F26)

Limoges saint figurine from Monks Eleigh, Suffolk, which appears to have been deliberately bent, probably during the Reformation. (PAS: SF-5EF445)

24. Altar piece, gilded and enamelled copper alloy, *c.* 1150 – *c.* 1300, from Shalfleet, Isle of Wight (IOW-680721).
Dimensions: 99.1 mm x 31.7 mm x 11.5 mm. Identified and recorded by Frank Basford.

One of the most remarkable examples of Limoges enamelling ever recorded with the Portable Antiquities Scheme is this item. It is not certain if it was once part of a cross, or furnished an altar-piece, or even was from a reliquary, but it is clearly the composite part of an important piece of medieval church-ware. The object is generally pentagonal, its top being surmounted by an orb, and a cross above. The back of the object shows that it was socketed to something else, probably held in place using a rivet through the hole on the front. The front shows a wonderfully executed winged figure rising from a cloud, probably an angel, but alternatively it could be the Evangelist symbol for St Matthew. Much of the light blue, red and white enamelling of the piece survives, as does some of the gilding, showing it once to have been a very beautiful object, fulfilling its task well of engaging with those participating in divine worship.

Limoges object, perhaps from an altar piece, found at Shalfleet, Isle of Wight. (PAS: IOW-680721)

25. Pyx lid, enamelled copper alloy, *c.* 1200 – *c.* 1300, from Arncliffe area, North Yorkshire (YORYM-58EB27).
Dimensions: 89.7 mm x 77.3 mm. Identified and recorded by Liz Andrews-Wilson, with Marian Campbell, John Cherry and Kevin Leahy.

This conical object is the lid from a medieval pyx, a receptacle used to contain the host (sacramental bread). Nowadays pyxes are used to transport sacramental bread to the ill or those otherwise attending Mass (the Eucharist). This might have been the case in the Middle Ages too, although many pyxes might simply have been containers for pre-consecrated bread. During the medieval period lay worshippers took communion less regularly than Christians do today, but it would have been important for the gravely ill or dying to take the blessed sacraments. This pyx is decorated with Limoges-style enamelling, though it is possibly of English manufacture. At its apex is a spherical collar, surmounted by a cross. The outside has been decorated with four roundels, each containing an eight-pointed star, coloured with greyish-blue and greyish-green enamel. Between each roundel are inscribed simple linear plant motifs, and there is incised and punched decoration elsewhere on the object. Otherwise much of the surface of the lid is gilded, both inside and out. Also apparent are two projecting loops, opposite one another, one serving as a hinge, the other as a means for keeping the vessel closed. The pyx lid was found together with two fragments of a late-medieval copper-alloy object, thought to be a crown, perhaps from a wooden statue (YORYM-5936A7). If this is the case, it seems likely that they were deposited together, perhaps during the Reformation.

Pyx lid from Arncliffe area, North Yorkshire. (PAS: YORYM-58EB27)

26. Tile, lead-glazed clay, *c.* 1250 – *c.* 1325, from Warkworth, Northamptonshire (BERK-8B90E8).
Dimensions: 114.58 mm x 112.35 mm x 23.1 mm. Identified and recorded by Anni Byard, with Julie Edwards, Maureen Mellor, Karen Slade and Ian Soden.

Glazed tiles were used to decorate the walking spaces of great churches, ecclesiastical buildings and important domestic dwellings. Of the many thousands made from the early thirteenth century, few survive in situ. Extant examples show diversity in design, with an array of subject matter considered appropriate for both religious and secular settings. This example from Warkworth shows a hunched male figure holding a staff, which he grips with both hands. The figure wears a long pointed hood or cowl, and has been interpreted as a jester or pilgrim; given the style of the hat the latter seems most likely. Parallels for this design include examples from the cloister pavement of Canterbury Cathedral and in Godmersham Church, Kent. It is known that such tiles were manufactured at Tyler Hill, Canterbury, in the late thirteenth and early fourteenth centuries, certainly before 1325, when these kilns stopped producing decorated floor tiles. The white coloured parts of the tile have been formed by stamping its design into its unfired fabric, which is then filled with white clay. The tile was then covered with a lead glaze and fired; combining the glazing and firing processes reduced labour costs. Still present on its sides and the underside can be seen white lime plaster, showing that the tile was probably laid as part of a large decorative scheme.

Clay tile showing a jester or pilgrim, from Warkworth, Northamptonshire. (PAS: BERK-8B90E8)

27. Pilgrim badge, lead alloy, *c.* 1300 – *c.* 1500, from the City of London (PUBLIC-364487).
Dimensions: 73.35 mm x 35 mm x 1.1 mm. Identified and recorded by Corneliu Thira.

Pilgrimage to holy sites and shrines became very popular in the Middle Ages, famously recounted by Geoffrey Chaucer in his *Canterbury Tales*. As these stories show, people of all walks of life would go on pilgrimage, not just those in holy orders or the very devout. At shrine sites, pilgrims would buy badges, such as this rather handsome lead-alloy example from the City of London, which they would then touch upon the relics of saints. It was believed that by doing so the miraculous properties of the saint in question would be transferred to the badge, and hence the badge wearer. Therefore, not only would the badge be a physical sign of pilgrimage (with its imagery helping to identify the saint prayed to), but it would also offer protection to its owner. One of the most important medieval saints was Archbishop Thomas (Becket) of Canterbury, brutally murdered in 1170 within his own cathedral. Those who killed the archbishop were four knights, acting after they heard King Henry II mutter frustrations about the insolence of his most senior cleric. It was an event that outraged Christendom, ensuring that Thomas (of somewhat dubious reputation previously) passed with ease to sainthood, and leaving King Henry's reputation in tatters. Pilgrims thenceforth flooded Canterbury to see its holy sites, including the bloodied murder weapon, the archbishop's episcopal gloves and the martyr's tomb, the latter being encrusted with jewels that had been sent to Canterbury by Europe's elite. The most popular

Left: Lead pilgrim badge commemorating the martyrdom of St Thomas, from the City of London. (PAS: PUBLIC-364487)

badges of St Thomas were of the bust reliquary that contained part of his skull, but a huge variety of other souvenirs were also made, including small bells inscribed with Thomas's name, a miniature sword that could be removed from its sheath, and even replicas of the aforementioned gloves. Openwork badges, such as this example, are rare survivors since they are fragile and easily damaged; this one only being saved in pristine condition because it was encased for nearly 700 years in the Thames mud. It does not have room to show all four of St Thomas's murderers, so the scene (common on an array of religious objects from across Europe) has been simplified to good effect. Note how the hand of God descends over the archbishop at the point of his martyrdom. Such badges, including their integral pin (see the badge's reverse), were created using moulds, the design being crafted into a soft stone such as limestone. The method allowed many badges to be made, quite cheaply and very quickly. That said, this badge appears to be unique, though it follows the style of examples that depict the death of St Alban.

Author making pilgrim badges, showing this to be a simple process!

28. Pendant, lead alloy, *c.* 1400 – *c.* 1550, from Hogsthorpe, Lincolnshire (LIN-FD4722).
Dimensions: 32 mm x 26 mm. Identified and recorded by Becky Sanderson.

This pendant is likely to have been purchased by a pilgrim visiting a holy site or shrine associated with St Margaret of Antioch. St Margaret was one of the most celebrated saints of the Middle Ages, one of the 'Fourteen Holy Helpers', venerated because of their particular efficacy. Her cult was once declared apocryphal by Pope Gelasius I (r. 492–6), but her popularity grew, especially following the Crusades. She offered sinners a full or partial remission of temporal punishment, which probably explained her popularity among ordinary (and God-fearing) people. The front of this pendant shows St Margaret, with a crossed staff, emerging from a dragon. The scene represents part of her legend where she was devoured by the devil, which came to her in the form of a dragon, only for the cross she was carrying to break the beast's innards so she could escape; similarly, in the Middle Ages it was thought a child was fortunate to escape its mother's belly alive, explaining why St Margaret was also evoked by those in childbirth. The back of the pendant has the Christogram IHS – an abbreviation of 'Jesus', but sometimes also transcribed as 'Jesus, saviour of mankind' – within a zig-zag border. Findspots of such pendants of St Margaret cluster in Lincolnshire, especially in the vicinity of Ketsby, likely to be associated with the former medieval church of St Margaret, where it is known an image of the saint was attracting offerings as late as 1529.

Lead pendant of St Margaret of Antioch, from Hogsthorpe, Lincolnshire. (PAS: LIN-FD4722)

St Margaret. (British Museum)

29. Badge, silver, *c.* 1500–30, from Preston, Lancashire (LANCUM-61F133).
Dimensions: 45 mm x 30 mm x 10 mm. Identified and recorded by Stuart Noon, with James Robinson and Michael Lewis.

An intriguing discovery from the North West is this badge, in the form of a female bust (in quarter profile) wearing early sixteenth-century dress, including a 'kennel-shaped' head-dress, with hair loose beneath. The low neckline of her dress reveals a cross-shaped pendant around her neck. On its reverse the badge has two extant stitching loops, one at the top behind the head and one in the left corner. A third loop is missing, but a scar remains where it was originally attached: such attachment loops may suggest it is of Continental manufacture. The object has been bent at a point close to its centre, and this may have been deliberate, perhaps an act of ritual or iconoclasm. It has been noted that the item resembles a South Netherlandish wooden bust reliquary of a female saint, thought to be a companion of St Ursula, now in the collections of the Metropolitan Museum of Art, New York. If this is the case (which is by no means certain) the object might have been bought by a pilgrim from Cologne, where St Ursula's Basilica holds relics of the saint and her companions; it was at Cologne, en route to Rome, that Ursula and 11,000 British virgins travelling with her were purportedly slaughtered by Huns.

Badge of St Ursula from Preston, Lancashire. (PAS: LANCUM-61F133)

30. Memorial plate, copper alloy, *c.* 1400 – *c.* 1500, from Wandsworth, Greater London (LON-3D2599).
Dimensions: 120.03 mm x 59.11 mm x 3.06 mm. Identified and recorded by Kate Sumnall, with Stephen Freeth.

A feature of many medieval parish churches across England are the memorials found on their flagstone floors. By the fifteenth century wealthy aristocrats could have commissioned large memorials of themselves (and their spouses) recumbent on tombs of stone or alabaster. Those less well-off, but by no means poor, may have had their likeness crafted on to brass and set into stone slabs on the floor. Such monuments, whatever their finery, had the same function – to remind the living to pray for their souls; the larger the memorial, the more likely they would be remembered and prayed for. Medieval people were convinced by the power of prayer and its practical benefits for the dead, whom they believed would progress through purgatory (an intermediary state between physical death and eternal life in heaven) through good deeds on earth, and the prayers of those who lived. Nowadays memorial brasses in churches are often covered to save them from wear and damage. It is not unusual to see the recesses in stone slabs that once bore brasses, but which are now lost. This example from the City of London is, with some lack of affection, called a 'waster'. It has been inscribed on both sides, probably highlighting immediate reuse of a wasted piece of brass. The Latin inscriptions, present on both sides, do not seem to relate to the same individual but are of similar date, hence it has been deduced an error was made, the brass discarded, and then (soon after) the object turned over and used for another memorial. One side tells us it was made for John (and his wife), asking God to absolve their souls: '[hic] iace(n)t Joh(ann)es d...' 'a(n)i(m)as absol[vat deus...]'. The other side was made for a son or daughter of a man and wife with the family name 'Warde'. They also ask for God's mercy. From the state of preservation, it is likely that the second side described was in fact the side used as a memorial.

Memorial brass from Wandsworth, Greater London. (PAS: LON-3D2599)

Impressive nineteenth-century recreation of Queen Eleanor of Castile's medieval tomb for her viscera at Lincoln. Eleanor was buried in three parts! (Author)

Church of St Giles Without, Cripplegate, City of London. Much of the church is medieval in date, but its tower was added later. (Andy Mabbett/Wikimedia Commons)

Chapter 4
Manufacture and Craftworking

An essential part of medieval life was the production of everyday goods, as well as some luxury items. All these objects were crafted by hand, with great skill and using relatively simple tools. It was the case that most craftworking was specialised, and in larger towns the outputs of tradesmen were regulated and protected by guilds; the most famous examples are the 'worshipful companies' of London, such as the goldsmiths, leathersellers and drapers' guilds. There was also a cottage industry, in which with people made and repaired goods at home, especially textiles and items of wood.

Late medieval re-enactor in his smithy. (Ros Tyrrell)

31. Matrix plate, copper alloy, *c.* 1300 – *c.* 1500, from Hursley, Hampshire (HAMP-8A5E03).
Dimensions: 43.95 mm x 35.2 mm x 3.2 mm. Identified and recorded by Rob Webley and Geoff Egan.

Some of the most intriguing discoveries recorded with the Portable Antiquities Scheme are those that demonstrate manufacture, even if the objects in themselves are relatively unsophisticated. This item is one such example. It is discoid, of fairly consistent thickness, but twice has been roughly cut diagonally, leaving around two thirds of the original disc. Both faces are considerably scratched, but one has two engraved devices upon it, very close to each other. The larger one is lozengiform with trefoil terminals on each corner, and within the field a fleur-de-lis; the upper half has a second border within the lozenge. The smaller device is more complex and shows an ornate fleur-de-lis, with three stems tied together and curved side petals. In its centre is a sub-triangular human face with clear features, flanked on either side by foliage, and with what appears to be another fleur-de-lis above. It might be that the object is simply a trial-piece or an open mould, but an alternative suggestion is that it is a matrix plate used for transferring motifs onto sheet metal. If this is the case then the craftsman would have gently hammered sheet-metal into the engraving, using a cushioning pad to soften the blows.

Matrix plate with two designs, from Hursley, Hampshire. (PAS: HAMP-8A5E03)

The fleur-de-lis was a very popular motif in the Middle Ages, as shown on this mount from Wetheringsett, Suffolk. (PAS: SF-735323)

32. Stamp, copper alloy, *c.* 1200 – *c.* 1400, from Clare, Suffolk (SF-B22470).
Dimensions: 37.36 mm x 35.56 mm x 6.81 mm. Identified and recorded by Andrew Brown.

The precise function of this fascinating item is uncertain. It may have served as a shallow mould for creating foil appliqués, presumably from gold or silver, or could have been used as a stamp to decorate materials such as leather. It is also possible that it formed one component of a larger mould or stamp. The fact that the object is incomplete, due to old breaks, makes it difficult to know how it was utilised, although it clearly had a manufacturing purpose. It is square in form, and rectangular in cross-section, with an elaborate motif upon one face. This comprises a circular border of multiple punched dots, at the centre of which is a lion rampant facing left, with its head turned to face the viewer. Its tail curves forwards, towards the middle of the beast's back, and its front paw is raised. Details of the animal's mane, hair on its lower limbs and tail, and other elements of the body, are picked out with multiple delicately incised grooves. The reverse of the object is flat and undecorated, but has a large circular concave moulding in one corner, with a shallow groove in another. The precise role of these indentations is uncertain, although they might indicate a means of attachment or method of using the object as a stamp or mould.

Right: Stamp or mould depicting a lion from Clare, Suffolk. (PAS: SF-B22470, Donna Wreathall)

Below: Drawing of the mount from Clare, Suffolk. (PAS: SF-B22470, Donna Wreathall)

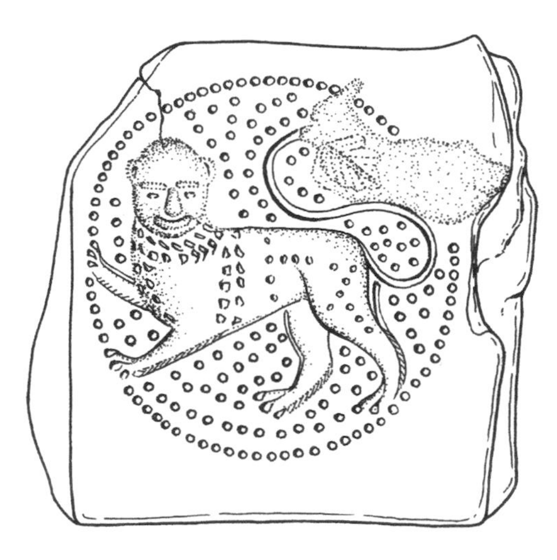

33. Seal matrix mould, copper alloy, *c.* 1300 – *c.* 1400, from Washingborough, Lincolnshire (LVPL-35AD66).
Dimensions: 28.2 mm x 20.11 mm x 11.23 mm. Identified and recorded by Vanessa Oakden, with Geoff Egan, Justine Bayley and Susan La Niece.

This valve from a three-part mould for making seal matrices is well crafted, and a rare find. Originally there would have been two side valves, of similar form, and a base; the latter was to prevent the molten metal from running out. At the centre of the rounded side of the object is a long projecting rod, which would have been used to pull the valves apart after casting. The recessed areas of the inner mould show that the matrices made from it had handles that were hexagonal in cross-section with rounded terminals. It is possible that a design on the flat bottom face of the matrix would have also been cast, though it is more likely that this would have been engraved afterwards, therefore allowing for a greater variety of designs to be manufactured. The mould is worn, a sign it was used multiple times, but its quality suggests it may have been the work of a goldsmith. The object has been subjected to scientific analysis, but no evidence of other material was found on its surface, and it is therefore not known what metal the matrices were made of; most matrices of this form appear to be copper alloy, but lead-alloy examples have been recorded with the Portable Antiquities Scheme.

Copper-alloy seal matrix mould from Washingborough, Lincolnshire. (PAS: LVPL-35AD66)

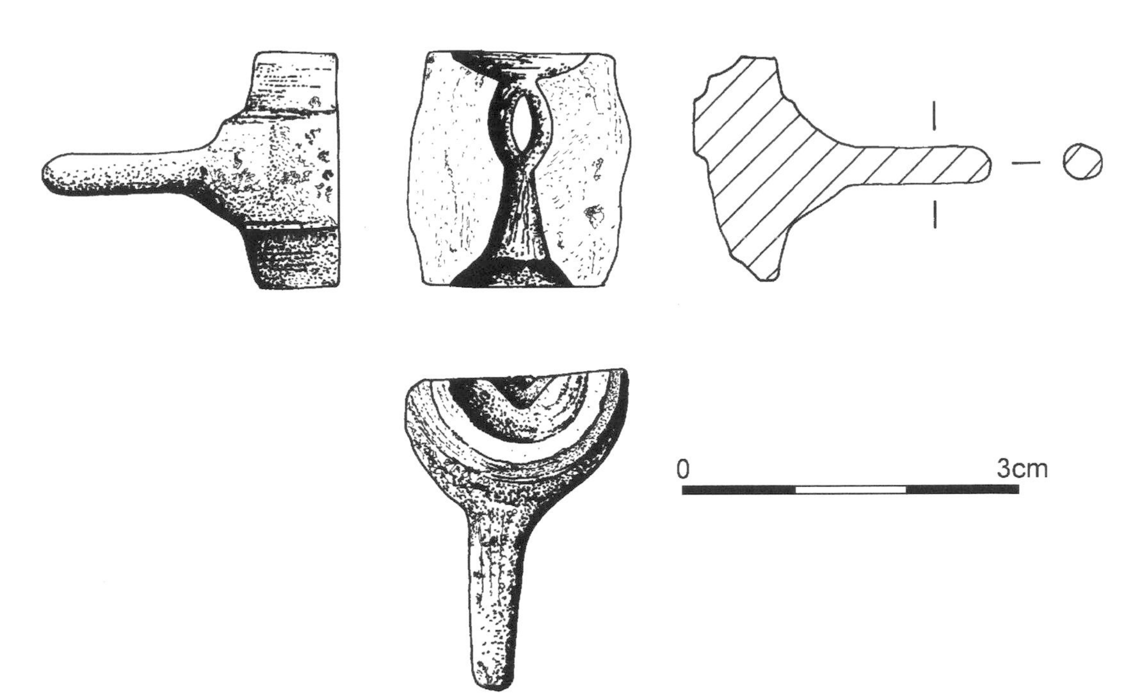

Above: Drawing of the seal matrix mould. (PAS: LVPL-35AD66, Susie White)

Right: Seal matrix with hexagonal handle and rounded terminal, similar to those made from the Washingborough mould. (PAS: HAMP-C015F6)

34. Mould, lead, *c.* 1427–30, from Faulkland, Somerset (SOM-0DF054).
Dimensions: 99.2 mm x 37.3 mm x 11.8 mm. Identified and recorded by Rob Webley, with Duncan Hook, Colin Torode and Michael Lewis.

Medieval England had a relatively sophisticated monetary system, able to produce good quality coinage, the circulation of which was highly regulated. This was important for ensuring confidence in the coinage minted, which was mostly silver, but with some gold issues. Nonetheless, clipping coins (to pass off sub-standard coinage and melt down the surplus) and producing fake coins are both apparent, although the penalties for those caught doing so were extremely harsh. Standard coins were produced by striking gold or silver blanks using dies charged to official moneyers, and therefore this lead object for producing a groat (four pence) appears to provide evidence for illegal coin manufacture. The object is of two parts, formed of flat rectangular bars, within which the impressions show the faces of a groat of Henry VI with a V-shaped longitudinal channel, presumably for the flow of liquid into the mould. The obverse depicts a crowned bust of the king, front-facing, within a nine-arched border and the inscription [hENRI]C [D]I G[RA] REX AnGL[I Z FRANC] (Henry, by the Grace of God, King of England and France). The reverse shows a long cross patty, dividing the field into quarters, with three pellets in each quarter, surrounded by the inscription (in two circles) +POSVI/ DEVm A/D[I]VTORE/ mEVm (I have made God my helper) // VIL/L[A]/ CALI/SIE (town of Calais). It is possible that the mould was used for casting in lead also, though it would have been a skill to achieve a melting point for the liquid lead alloy without damaging the mould. It is also unclear how easy the coins made from it might have been passed off as regular coinage; these moulds were found with another (SOM-0EC771), possibly for a halfpenny of Edward III. Another, albeit unlikely, possibility is that the object could have been used to make amulets, such as those associated with the unofficial cult of Henry VI, whose sainthood was (unsuccessfully) promoted by Lancastrians. Alternatively, and more likely, the moulds could have been used to make wax coins, from which moulds could have been produced for metal forgeries.

Coin mould for groat of Henry VI, from Faulkland, Somerset. (PAS: SOM-0DF054)

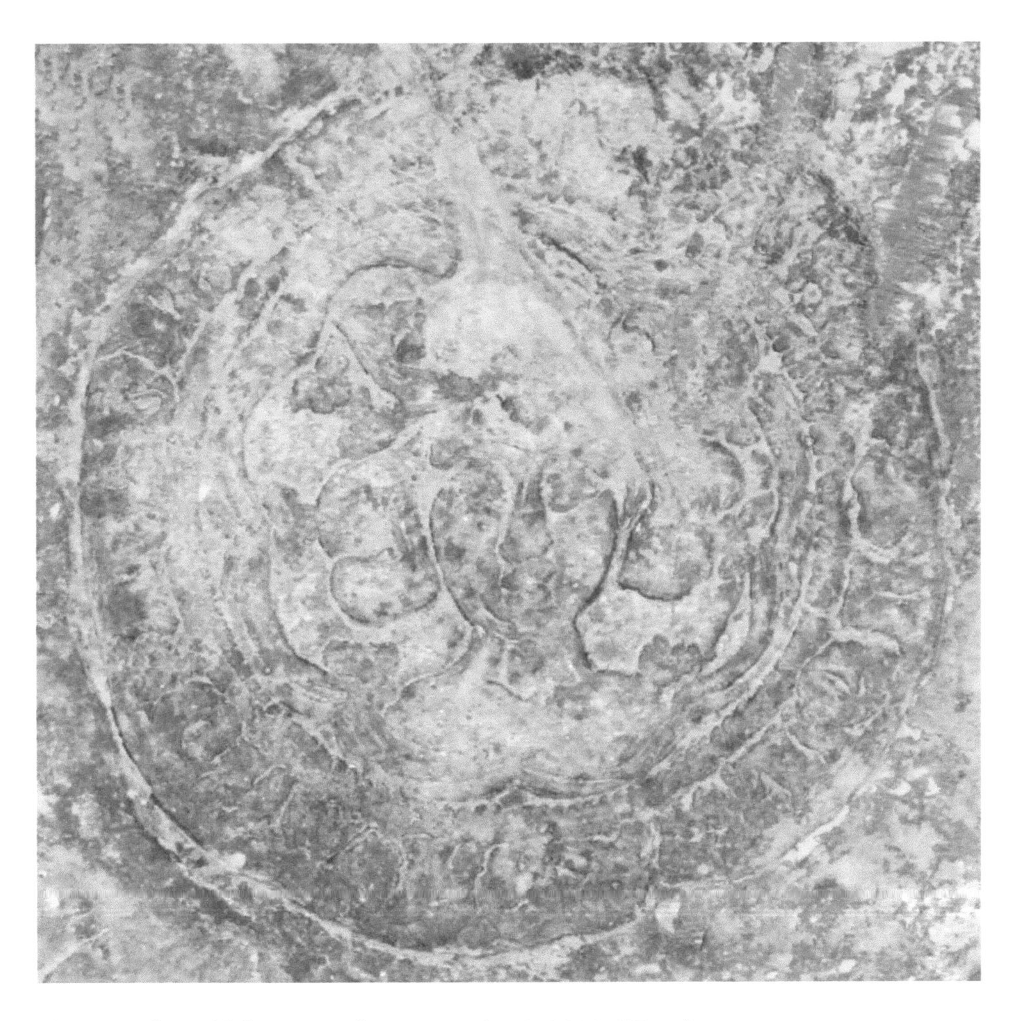

Close up of mould for groat of Henry VI. (PAS: SOM-0DF054)

Groat of Henry VI minted in London, from the Isle of Wight. (PAS: IOW-D6C2EC)

Pilgrim badge of Henry VI. (British Museum)

35. Axe, iron, *c.* 1300 – *c.* 1500, from Potters Bar, Furzefield, Hertfordshire (BH-E23E57).
Dimensions: 178 mm x 92 mm x 38.5 mm. Identified and recorded by Julian Watters, with Kevin Leahy.

Axes were used in war, but were also a common tool used both by craftsmen and as everyday objects for felling and cutting wood. Some axes had the shaft off-set (slightly angled), as might be the case here, so that the person using it could produce a flat surface without constantly banging their knuckles. Given most axeheads are made of iron, medieval examples are rare. This one is of sub-triangular cross-section and contains what appears to be the mineralised remains of the wooden shaft, held in place by an iron wedge. It is therefore an interesting and important survivor. The butt is roughly vertical, the upper side of the socket is convex and slopes upwards, towards the blade, and there is a pronounced lip at its base. The thickness of the blade gradually tapers towards the convex cutting edge. The upper side of the blade is straight, gradually sloping upwards, while the underside has a pronounced concavity, with its lower corner located well below the base of the socket. This form of axe is sometimes referred to as a 'bearded axe' and is often associated with the Viking period. However, it is a form that continued through time, with a peak of use in the high to late Middle Ages, from which this example perhaps dates.

Iron axe from Potters Bar, Furzefield, Hertfordshire. (PAS: BH-E23E57)

Manuscript illustration of a man felling trees with an axe. (British Library)

Chapter 5
Domestic Life

The finds recorded with the Portable Antiquities Scheme provide unique insights into domestic life during the Middle Ages, which is especially important given that the life of most people is otherwise absent from history. What we learn from these objects is that people owned more than we might expect, but most of these possessions were utilitarian, enabling them to have some comforts in what otherwise must have been for most a very harsh and uncertain environment to live. Playthings are also recorded, showing there was a lighter side to life and that people took time to enjoy one another's company.

Re-enactor spinning. The spindle whorl can be clearly seen. (Ros Tyrrell)

36. Spindle whorl, lead, *c.* 1300 – *c.* 1400, from Upton-by-Chester, Cheshire (LVPL-1D218E).
Dimensions: 29.3 mm x 10 mm. Identified and recorded by Ben Jones and Vanessa Oakden.

Spindle whorls are extremely common metal-detector finds, though they are often hard to date since many are of basic form and undecorated. They provide an essential component of the spinning process, used on spindles to increase and maintain the speed of the spin when producing thread from wool, cotton, flax and suchlike. This example is lead, but they are found made of different materials, including copper alloy and pottery. It has upon it a pattern of zigzags creating triangular enclosures, each filled with a pellet. It is a design that helps date it to the Middle Ages.

Spindle whorl from Upton-by-Chester, Cheshire. (PAS: LVPL-1D218E)

Late medieval spindle whorl made of pottery, found in the City of London. (PAS: LON-370317)

37. Thimble, copper alloy, *c.* 1400 – *c.* 1550, from Claverley, Shropshire (WMID-CE672D).
Dimensions: 18.33 mm x 2.02 mm. Identified and recorded by Victoria Allnatt.

Thimbles are one of the humblest objects made, but were of essential importance to domestic work in the medieval period. Many thousands were made, and they are frequent metal-detector finds. This example is complete, although it has suffered some damage. It is broadly domed in form, with its walls flaring outwards towards the rim. The indentations (pits) are smaller on the top than on the walls. They are arranged in a spiral band and are relatively evenly spaced. Such thimbles were made over a long period of time, but similar examples have been dated to the latter part of the Middle Ages. They are of a type commonly known as beehive thimbles, but they are also described as 'heavy duty'. Although thimbles are synonymous with textile working, particularly sewing, their application may have been much wider, protecting the fingers in an array of work.

Beehive thimble from Claverley, Shropshire. (PAS: WMID-CE672D)

38. Mount, copper alloy, *c.* 1175 – *c.* 1350, from the Deverills, Wiltshire (WILT-CE97F3).
Dimensions: 36.96 mm x 24.13 mm x 2.78 mm. Identified and recorded by Jane Hanbidge.

It is not known to what this openwork mount was once attached, but its rectangular form might suggest use on a piece of furniture, such as a chest or casket. It shows a beast, perhaps a deer, standing right, and looking back over itself. Also apparent is some scrolled foliate decoration, perhaps representing the woodland within which the animal would have lived. Unfortunately, the mount is incomplete, with roughly 30 per cent missing. It has the remains of gilding, showing it to be an exquisite embellishment of some importance. During the Middle Ages, people would have used chests and caskets for many of their belongings, including clothes, as well as jewellery and other personal items. Medieval forest laws regulated who might hunt deer and other prized animals, and therefore these beasts became popular motifs in art, especially among the highest social echelons.

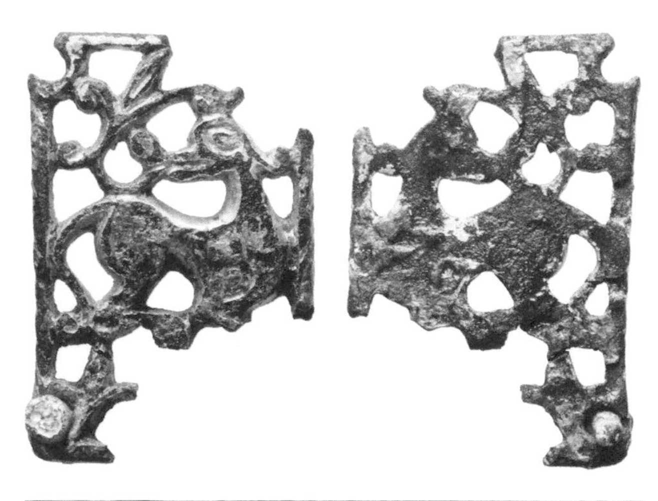

Zoomorphic mount, perhaps from a chest or casket, found in the Deverills, Wiltshire. (PAS: WILT-CE97F3)

Deer in woodland. (Author)

39. Zoomorphic padlock, copper alloy, *c.* 1200 – *c.* 1400, from Pickering, North Yorkshire (YORYM-BA035A).
Dimensions: 42 mm x 33.6 mm x 13.7 mm. Identified and recorded by Gail Hitchens.

Medieval people were as concerned as we are today to keep precious things safe under lock and key. Padlocks survive in several main types, of which those operated with a slide key are found in significant numbers. These are usually of cylindrical form, giving rise to the name 'barrel' padlock. An intriguing phenomenon of the Middle Ages are examples of these locks in the form of animals, in this case a stylised three-dimensional horse. Clearly defined are the horse's facial features, harness and saddle. The object is hollow, so that it can operate as a lock. In the animal's chest is an oval hole, through which the key would have been inserted; in this case it has ruptured. The hind quarters of the horse have three square holes (one positioned above the other two) through which the padlock mechanism would have engaged with the cylindrical case. The lock would have operated by joining the barrel and mechanism together. A key would have then been used to close the springs on the mechanism, allowing the barrel to be removed. The diversity of padlocks from the Middle Ages suggests that locksmiths probably did not share details of their manufacture, as might be expected with security devices. Most padlocks, especially the smaller ones, were probably used to secure chests and caskets, rather than doors.

Zoomorphic padlock from Pickering, North Yorkshire. (PAS: YORYM-BA035A)

40. Vessel handle, copper alloy, *c.* 1300 – *c.* 1500, from Watlington, Oxfordshire (BH-EEE305).
Dimensions: 60.3 mm x 48.4 mm x 22.8 mm. Identified and recorded by Julian Watters, with Harvey Cross.

Beautifully crafted, this solid-cast figurine is in the form of a seated dog. The animal is well-moulded and of realistic, if slightly stylised, appearance; its head, in particular, is overly large and has caricatured features. The animal is seated in an upright, somewhat cramped position, with its tail raised – one theory is that it is shown defecating! Its feet rest upon a roughly rectangular base, the underside of which bears traces of solder and also numerous linear punch-marks; these would have helped to secure it in place. It is likely, then, that this figurine decorated a larger object, probably serving as a vessel handle. Hexagonal flat lids with handles formed of squatting dogs have been found during archaeological excavations in London, all made of pewter. It has been suggested that these are from salt containers, and that maybe the dog had a special significance as the guardian of food, or salt in particular. Similar vessels have upon them the inscription CUM SIS IN MENSA PRIMO DE PAPAVERE PENSO (when you are at the table think first of the poor), a reminder that few medieval people had the wealth for such luxurious living.

Vessel-handle in the form of a dog, from Watlington, Oxfordshire. (PAS: BH-EEE305)

41. Lamp hanger, copper alloy, *c.* 1100 – *c.* 1300, from Goring, Oxfordshire (SUR-217AC4).
Dimensions: 32.56 mm x 25.87 mm. Identified and recorded by David Williams.

It is easy to forget how dark life could be in the Middle Ages, especially during wintertime when days were short. The fireside would have probably been the main source of light for most in the evenings, but candles (see 42) and oil burners would also have been used. Medieval houses, being mostly made of organic materials, were vulnerable to combustion. Death inquests show that fire was very dangerous to life, with people succumbing to fireside accidents and unattended flames; the young and the old, in particular, being harmed and killed. Oil lamps were sometimes suspended, as demonstrated by this fascinating find of a probable lamp hanger. It is roughly cast in the form of a hollow openwork pyramid. At its top is a rounded apex loop for suspension, perhaps so it could hang from a celling beam. At its base there is a rounded loop in each angle, from which the lamp (probably made of glass or ceramic) would have been suspended, perhaps using metal chains. No clear parallels for the object have been found, but it is similar in form to three-armed lamp hangers, also of medieval date.

Above: Common form of lamp hanger, from Ashen, Essex. (PAS: ESS-E401E3)

Left: Lamp hanger from Goring, Oxfordshire. (PAS: SUR-217AC4)

42. Candleholder, copper alloy, *c.* 1300 – *c.* 1400, from the Deverills, Wiltshire (WILT-21F000).
Dimensions: 123.68 mm x 56.77 mm x 18.09 mm. Identified and recorded by Alyson Tanner.

Medieval candles were either made of tallow, which was cheap but gave off a foul odour, or beeswax, which was expensive but sweet smelling. Oil (as noted above, see 41) offered an alternative, but the smell would vary, depending on the quality of the oil used. Candleholders came in a variety of forms, but either had a cup, to hold the candle, or a prick, upon which it was spiked. Likewise, candleholders might have stands, bases or prickets. The example here is of the latter type, but is a folding candle, presumably so that it could be easily transported or conveniently stored. It is of simple type, comprising a cup for the candle, a stem and a pivoting spike; the spike would have enabled it to be thrust into a wooden beam or table. It is unusual in that it is made completely of sheet metal, with the baseless cup being riveted to the stem. The only decoration on the object is three sets of punched indentations forming cross-like designs. It is not known how reliable this form of candleholder was, as there must have been a risk (with its pivoting join) that it might fall over, especially when top-heavy.

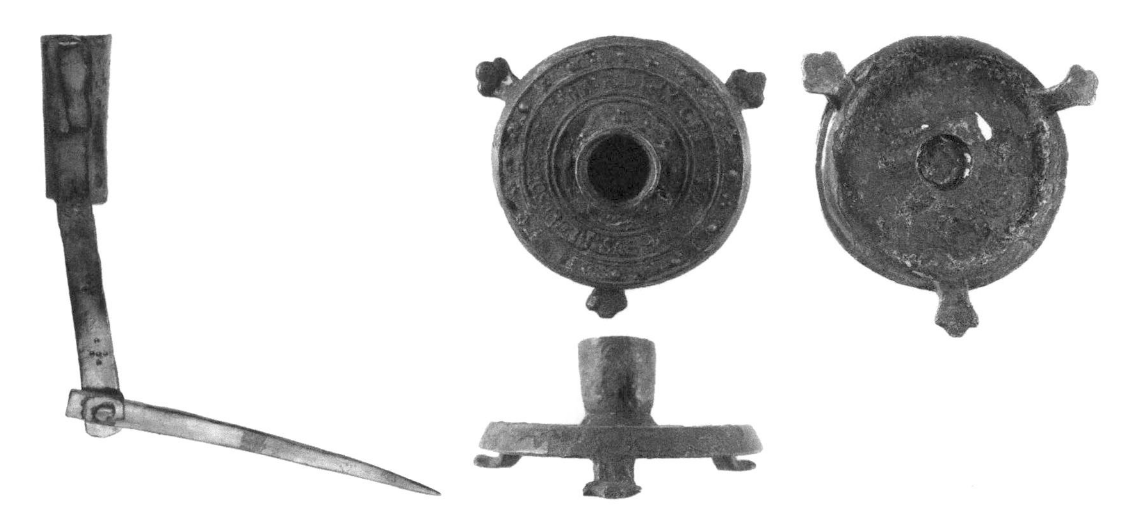

Above left: Pivoting candleholder from the Deverills, Wiltshire. (PAS: WILT-21F000)

Above right: Medieval candleholder from the City of London (LON-6C500D) with an inscription asking for God's protection. (PAS)

43. Knife, iron, wood and copper alloy, *c.* 1400 – *c.* 1500, from Greenwich, London (KENT-8A4D03).
Dimensions: 95.69 mm x 15.76 mm x 7.8 mm. Identified and recorded by Jo Ahmet.

This knife is another remarkable find from the River Thames foreshore (see 9, 17 and 27), but down-river from the City. Given that such knives normally consist of organic materials and iron, they normally only survive in waterlogged conditions. This example is incomplete, with only the wooden handle, with copper-alloy fittings and iron tang, remaining; perhaps the blade was lost in antiquity. The circular copper-alloy rivets are not purely decorative, but actually fix the handle to the blade; between them are clover-like trefoils on each side. Also surviving is the trefoil pommel, which helps date the find. In the Middle Ages such knives would have been commonplace, carried by people both to eat with (forks were not ordinarily used) and used as tools, much like a penknife today.

Knife from Greenwich, London. (PAS: KENT-8A4D03)

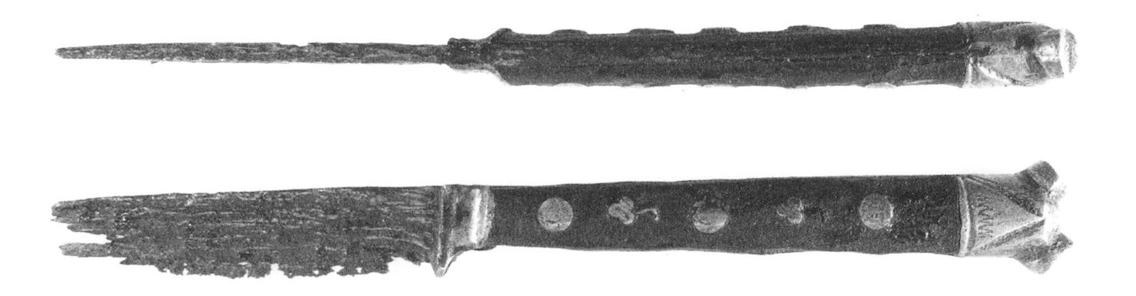

Late medieval knife from the City of London. (PAS: LON-6EAAD0)

44. Flute or whistle, bone, from Southwark, London (LON-58D1C9).
Dimensions: 153.65 mm x 25.39 mm. Identified and recorded by Ben Paites, with Hazel Forsyth. Acquired by the Museum of London.

Musical instruments were much enjoyed in the Middle Ages, and chance finds of them are extremely rare. This example is of primitive form, being carved from a tibia, probably from a sheep or goat. The bone is cylindrical, flaring at one end to form a trefoil. The calcareous material in the centre of the bone has been removed, in order to form the channel for the pipe. At the flared end, the cork fipple (block) is still in situ creating the blow-hole, though it is not clear whether it has the necessary breathing slot due to its condition; fipples were used to regulate the breath passing through the instrument and are rarely found in place. The square perforation on the shin side of the bone served as a finger-hole, ensuring the instrument had a pitch. Since the object has no thumb or tone holes, it might be better described as a whistle. It is thought it might be possible for it to achieve a double octave.

Flute from Southwark, London.
(PAS: LON-58D1C9)

Above: Re-enactors playing medieval music. (Author)

Right: Women playing music in a medieval manuscript. (British Library)

45. Miniature fuddling-cup, copper alloy, *c.* 1400 – *c.* 1600, from York, North Yorkshire (YORYM-6DD481).
Dimensions: 39.6 mm x 38.9 mm x 24.5 mm. Identified and recorded by Rebecca Griffiths.

Throughout time, children and adults alike have had playthings to occupy their time for fun and relaxation. The medieval period was no different, but finds of toys are not common: it was probably the case that most playthings were simply made or constructed of material which is unlikely to survive, or that children repurposed other items as toys or played with natural objects, such as sticks, stones and nuts. Fuddling-cups are not particularly rare, but are intriguing finds, and certainly highlight the fact that medieval people had a sense of fun. This object is in the form of three miniature cups or cauldrons that are joined together as a single piece. Each vessel has a flared rim, waisted neck and curved bulbous body with a flat base. Two of the vessels retain single legs, with outward turned feet; all that remains of the other leg is its stump. The vessels all have handles, though one is damaged. Such miniature fuddling-cups replicate full-size ceramic versions, which often also have holes in their walls. They were designed to contain liquid that was (it seems) impossible to drink without spilling, and therefore were a source of entertainment, much like in a modern drinking game. It is not certain whether these smaller versions served the same purpose or not. Perhaps they were just used by children mimicking adults' play.

Miniature fuddling-cup from York, North Yorkshire. (PAS: YORYM-6DD481)

Above: Kings playing chess in a medieval manuscript. (British Library)

Right: Gaming piece, probably for chess, from Southwark, London. (PAS: LON-55F862)

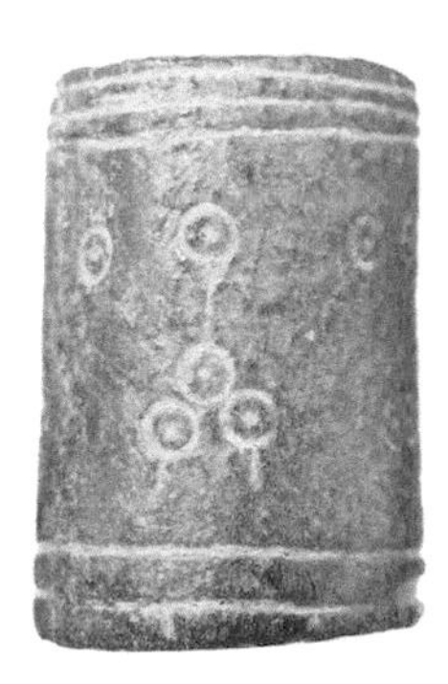

Chapter 6
Commerce and Literacy

The Middle Ages experienced increased urbanisation, but it was still the case that most people lived in the countryside. Fairs and markets became commonplace, enabling goods to travel from the countryside to towns and vice versa. These items might be transported by land, but also by navigable rivers and the sea; ships were essential for moving bulk goods. England's ports ensured trade with Continental Europe and beyond, giving rise to a mercantile class. Payments could be made with cash (predominately silver coinage) or through the provision of goods. Although this was a period when most people could not read nor write, the written word was vitally important and necessary for legal and commercial transactions.

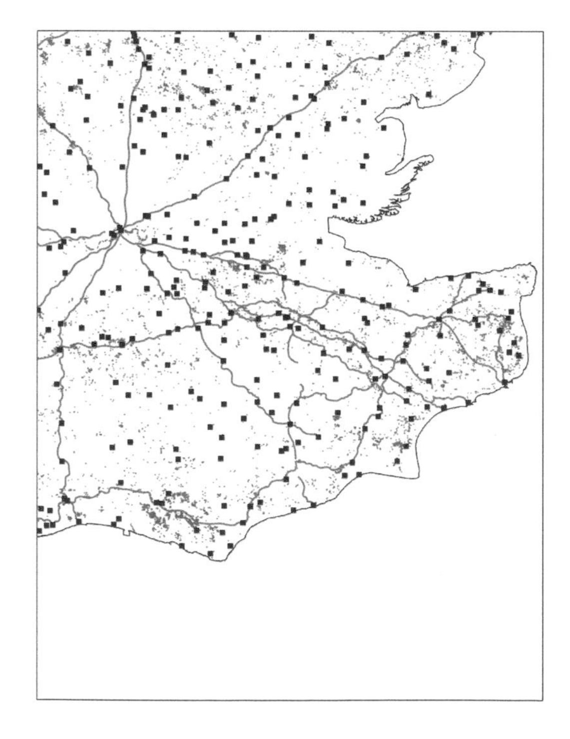

Map of south-east England, showing the proximity of medieval finds recorded by the Portable Antiquities Scheme with known market sites. (Eljas Oksanen)

46. Cloth seal, lead alloy, *c.* 1300 – *c.* 1550, from Woodnesborough, Kent (KENT-9A9391).
Dimensions: 28.3 mm x 3.7 mm. Identified and recorded by Jennifer Jackson, with Geoff Egan.

Cloth seals are unassuming objects, often found incomplete or damaged, but are immensely important for understanding the medieval cloth trade and the regulation of it. In many towns, including London, the trade in textiles was strictly regulated, ensuring not only that the appropriate tax was paid (known in England as alnage), but also that only the highest quality textiles were sold; this essentially protected official manufacturers from the competition of inferior products. Leaden seals were also applied to cloth by wardens or searchers of textile craft guilds to show that they were of high standard. These not only related to how they were made (the quality of the cloth), but also the dyeing process. Wool could be exported from Yorkshire, worked into cloth in Flanders and then dyed in London; therefore cloth seals tell of the movement of these textiles across much of north-west Europe, particularly between England and the Low Countries. This example was issued by alnagers (the officials who inspected the quality of cloth) in the city of Bristol. The obverse shows a ship sailing from a castle port (the city arms), with the legend [S' SVB]CIDII x PNNORV x around (subsidy of cloth). The reverse design has a crowned leopard's head with fleur-de-lis in its mouth, and the legend S' VLNAGII x P[AN]NORV x IN * BRISTOLIE (seal of the alnage of cloth in Bristol).

Cloth seal issued in Bristol, from Woodnesborough, Kent. (PAS: KENT-9A9391)

Left: Cloth seal, probably issued in northern France, but found in Durham. Upon it is the imprint of the fabric to which it was attached. (PAS: PUBLIC-438A85)

Below: Sheep were important to the medieval trade in cloth. (Author)

47. Purse bar, copper alloy, *c.* 1400 – *c.* 1600, from Swynnerton, Staffordshire (WMID-2CEDB9).
Dimensions: 57.7 mm x 45.7 mm x 9.2 mm. Identified and recorded by Helen Glenn, with Teresa Gilmore.

Like people nowadays, medieval men and women carried money about their person. Contemporary costumes, as far as we can tell, did not usually have pockets, and therefore money and valuables were transported about in purses. These, made of leather, usually hung from the belt, suspended using a metal bar and frame. The Portable Antiquities Scheme has recorded numerous examples of varying form and design, many incomplete or fragmentary, some decorated and others not. Rarely do the leather or textile purses themselves survive, only the metal parts that held them together and that allowed them to be suspended. The example highlighted here is quite small. It consists of two parts that survive, a bar and suspension loop. A small fragment of the frame, which looped around the leather purse, is also present, secured to the bar by its rove. Only the central block of the purse bar is decorated, with an engraved saltire. Other examples recorded have inscriptions, normally religious, such as words from the Ave Maria prayer.

Purse bar from Swynnerton, Staffordshire. (PAS: WMID-2CEDB9)

Above: Fragment of a purse bar with religious inscription, from Dorrington, Lincolnshire. (PAS: LIN-160CFD)

Left: Replica leather purse being worn. (Author)

48. Jetton, copper alloy, *c.* 1461–97, from Cothelstone, Somerset (SOM-1BA109).
Dimensions: 26.16 mm x 2.56 mm. Identified and recorded by Julie Shoemark.

Jettons are found in significant numbers, of various types and varieties. They include both English-made examples and pieces imported from the Continent. Most medieval jettons were reckoning counters, for financial calculations, but it is not implausible that some had a wider use, such as gaming pieces or small change, as was the case from the seventeenth century. This jetton is not unique or particularly unusual (indeed, another example of the same type was found nearby: SOM-1BC3F4), but it is well preserved. It was minted in Tournai (modern-day Belgium), and is contemporaneous with the reigns of Louis XI (r. 1461–83) and Charles VIII (r. 1483–98) of France. It is thicker than many other jettons, and therefore might be a piedfort, the exact function of which remains unclear. Upon its obverse is the Christogram IHS (see 28) in Gothic script, surrounded by flowers. The reverse has a cross fleuretty with flowers in its angles. Both sides have the inscription AVE MARIA STELLA DEI MATER, the first lines of a liturgical prayer honouring the Virgin Mary, as star of the sea and mother of God.

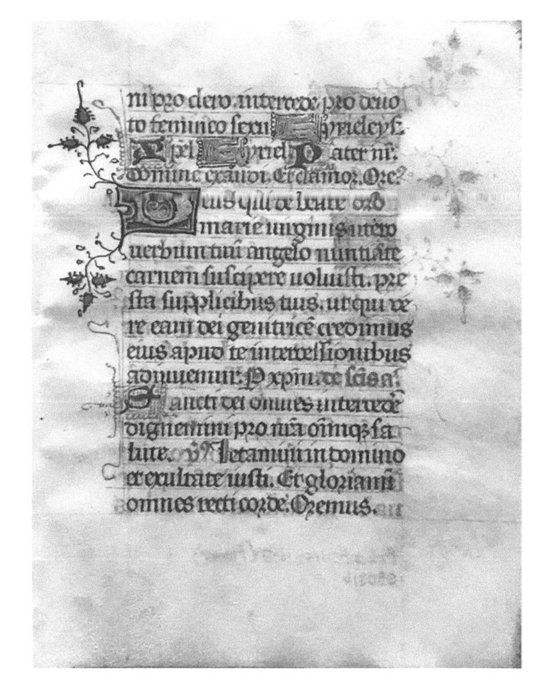

Above: Tournai jetton with prayer to the Virgin Mary, from Cothelstone, Somerset. (PAS: SOM-1BA109)

Right: Prayer honouring Mary in a medieval manuscript. (Author)

49. Seal matrix, copper alloy, *c.* 1250 – *c.* 1300, from Stockbridge, Hampshire (HAMP-FE2B25).
Dimensions: 33.1 mm x 21.23 mm x 8.33 mm. Identified and recorded by Katie Hinds, with Mary Chester-Kadwell and Laura Burnett.

Seal matrices identifiably belonging to women are infrequent but important discoveries, revealing significant information about the role of women in landownership and other legal agreements necessitating the use of seals. Pointed oval matrices, such as this example, mostly date to the second half of the thirteenth century. They are a type apparently favoured by women, though many recorded by the Portable Antiquities Scheme were owned by men, challenging this view. The matrix shows a female figure standing, facing forwards, and wearing a headdress, long skirt with long sleeves, and a cloak fastened across her chest by a cord or chain. Her dress is not fitted at the top, a fashion which also helps date the object. Her right arm is clasped to the chest while the left holds a hawk. Below the hawk is a hare or rabbit, apparently hanging and probably dead, presumably caught by the hawk. Around the edge of the seal is the inscription S' BEATRICIE : W[A...]EnSIS (seal of Beatrice W[al]ensis or W[ar]ensis); Walensis is not an uncommon family name, originally designating a 'foreigner', but by this time meaning 'Welsh'. It has not been possible to learn anything more about Beatrice Walensis/Warensis from written records.

Seal matrix of Beatrice Walensis from Stockbridge, Hampshire. (PAS: HAMP-FE2B25)

Medieval manuscript illustration showing a king with a sealed document. (British Library)

50. Gulden of the Bishopric of Liège, gold, 1482–1505, from Ivinghoe area, Buckinghamshire (BUC-ED8235).
Dimensions: 21.8 mm. Recorded and identified by Ros Tyrrell, with Barrie Cook.

Pierced coins are fascinating discoveries, since they shed light on the life story of an object. Sometimes coins were pierced so that they could be made into jewellery, such as pendants or similar; there are numerous examples on the Portable Antiquities Scheme database, including coins made into brooches. Given that the piercing on this coin is not aligned with its design it has been suggested that it might have been pierced to test its quality, since during this time gulden of Liège (such as this) were known to be of relatively poor-quality gold compared to other European coins. This example was minted in the name of John de Horne, Bishop of Liège (1482–1505). Its obverse shows the bishop's arms, surrounded by the inscription IOhS DE HORN EPS LEODIE (John de Horne, Bishop of Liège). The reverse has a figure of St Lambert as a bishop, with the inscription SANCTVS LAMBERTV (St Lambert). The medieval cathedral of Liège was dedicated to St Lambert, its bishop, who was martyred there.

Gulden of the Bishop of Liège, from Ivinghoe area, Buckinghamshire. (PAS: BUC-ED8235)

Brooch made from a medieval coin minted in Rome, found at Great Munden, Hertfordshire. (PAS: BH-75AB13)

Further Reading

Clark, J. (ed.), 1995, *The Medieval Horse and its Equipment: Medieval Finds from Excavations in London* 5 (HMSO: London).

Egan, G. & Pritchard, F., 1991, *Dress Accessories c. 1150 – c. 1450: Medieval Finds from Excavations in London* 3 (HMSO: London).

Egan, G., 1998, *The Medieval Household, Daily Living c. 1150 – c. 1450: Medieval Finds from Excavation in London* 6 (Stationary Office: London).

Kelleher, R., 2015, *A History of Medieval Coinage in England: Illustrated by Coins in the Fitzwilliam Museum*, Cambridge (Greenlight Publishing: Witham).

Lewis, M., 2014, *Saints and their Badges: Saints' Lives and Medieval Pilgrim Badges* (Greenlight Publishing: Witham).

Saunders, P. & Saunders, E. (eds.), 1991, *Medieval Catalogue: Salisbury & South Wiltshire Museum* 1 (Salisbury & South Wiltshire Museum: Salisbury).

Saunders, P. (ed.), 1991, *Medieval Catalogue: Salisbury & South Wiltshire Museum* 3 (Salisbury & South Wiltshire Museum: Salisbury).

Saunders, P. (ed.), 2012, *Medieval Catalogue: Salisbury & South Wiltshire Museum* 4 (Salisbury & South Wiltshire Museum: Salisbury).

Spencer, B., 2001, *Medieval Catalogue: Salisbury & South Wiltshire Museum* 2 (Salisbury & South Wiltshire Museum: Salisbury).

Bodiam Castle, East Sussex, one of England's prettiest medieval castles. (Author)

About the author

Dr Michael Lewis is Head of Portable Antiquities & Treasure at the British Museum. He has an interest in medieval small finds, particularly those associated with religious devotion, but is probably best known for his work on the Bayeux Tapestry and has been instrumental in its proposed loan to the United Kingdom in 2022. Michael is a Fellow of the Society of Antiquaries of London, a Member of the Chartered Institute for Archaeologists and a Liveryman of the Worshipful Company of Art Scholars.